MW00986894

IT'S ABOUT THYME

Jamaican Recipes from the Heart

2nd edition

Printed in the United States of America.

ISBN: 978-1-59571-249-3
Library of Congress Control Number: 2008920112

Word Association Publishers
205 5th Avenue
Tarentum, PA 15084
www.wordassociation.com

THAT'S NANNY WITH MY HUSBAND, STEVE

PREFACE

Like many of my life experiences, I did not know at the time where my first trip to Jamaica would take me. For so long, it was something of a dream, a faraway place where rainbows kiss the horizon, a childhood memory from the learning channel. In my dreams, Jamaica is a place where night meets day and merges into a magical and eternal love affair. I remember the anticipation building inside of me as the months and days grew closer. My stagnation soon turned into a conscious obsession, a subconscious remedy for the blues. My mind was possessed with expectation and a strange longing. Finally, the day would be at hand, and if I knew then what I know now, I would have left sooner for this date with the exotic.

I arrived late, a fitting torture for an impatient soul. The bumpy ride on a crowded bus did nothing for my senses. My taste buds were numb from biting my tongue, my favorite medicine for my fear of flying. I remember the blind feeling I had as I tried to peer into the dark Caribbean night. The feeling shifting more to disappointment as the vessel sailed on. This must have been what Christopher Columbus felt hundreds of years ago when he first experienced the Island. Just as Mr. Columbus, I came too far to turn back. There was an exciting energy brewing, hard to understand then in the tropic-soaked darkness, but it was there. It was the marrying sound of my beating heart with the backdrop of alluring evening sounds. The visual beauty of the island was hidden from me. I would have to wait one more night.

The night melted away under the embracing arms of the sun. Its fingers flirted warmly on my brow, gently welcoming me out of unconsciousness. I opened my eyes that morning and saw the world for the first time. I awoke and hypnotically followed the direction of the sun as its golden rays called out to me. With exasperation I quickly inhaled and drew open the blinds of destiny. The sands of the hourglass stopped for a moment, as I was engulfed with the senses of the New World. With a sobering breath I gulped and attempted to take in this strange yet beautiful elixir. It was overwhelming. I fell into a drunken state of sights and sounds, which blended perfectly with the morning sun, all the time the sun never leaving my side as it slowly melted away my inhibitions. Darkness was replaced with light. The challenge would be to spend the next two weeks soaking it in.

I would leave this place a changed person, with a great appreciation of where the term "One Love" originated. Jamaica is the perfect ongoing blend of family, food, and love, mixed with a hypnotic island beat and stirred in a huge melting pot of cultural diversity and world history. It was from this enlightening experience that I realized Jamaica was not a New World after all; instead, an old, friendly one with many colorful and tantalizing stories. It became necessary to tell my story, not rewrite history, in a form that I know and love the best, FOOD. It would become old meets new, who both meet me, and I hope to introduce them to you through my unique blend of old and new twists on Jamaican food. It was the dawn of all awakenings and I was a baby to the beauty of an island I would eventually call home. So this is my story, and "It's about thyme!"

INTRODUCTION

Family has always been an important force in my life. I come from a family of four kids, with me nestled somewhere in the middle. I could ramble on about how excruciating it was being a middle child, but in retrospect it was fitting. It was the perfect mix of being spoiled and scolded. It was equilibrium of free things given to me by my older siblings and then having them broken or taken by my younger brother Vito. One of my favorite gifts in grade school was from my older brother Frank ... a "submarine," a confusing play on words for a grade school girl at the time, a foreshadow for a future episode. To my lucky disappointment, it was food. Coming from a modest background, the free lunches were far and few between. However, far and few made for cool and courageous lunch breaks, opposite the mundane schoolyard games. With my school situated in a metropolis of fast foods, it was just a matter of time before my appreciation of free food turned to a love for the rich savor of cooking and the magic of spices.

Raised at the corner of Bloor and Euclid, I grew up in the heart of the city, in our humble three-story semi-detached home, surrounded by a coffee shop, variety store, and alleyway. Everything I wanted was a stone's throw away, including my best friend, Rita Galati, who lived across the street from me. Rita and I would spend summers together on our verandas, rotating as the shade shifted from my side of the street to hers. We never ventured far as children, but we were bold in our barefoot escapades. We created an adventure for every passerby, connecting stories to the faces and saving them as keepsakes for future laughs. That was the beauty of living downtown; you were never bored, because the faces were always different. If we weren't busy inventing stories, we were trying to find enough money to buy one of our favorite things to eat, fortune cookies. We would sit in Rita's backyard and devour a whole bag of cookies. Boy, did we like to eat, and still do. The streets were painted a brilliant rainbow of cultures. To the south of us was little Italy; to the north was little Korea. My closest neighbors were Trinie, Indian, Italian, Korean, and Greek. The collage of foods from these homes was larger than life and kept me fascinated. The lettuce was always greener on the other side of the semi. I loved the streets, the faces, and the stories, but I can't say the same about my house.

My house had more rooms than actual space, and no matter how empty it was it always seemed crowded. Despite the rooms, I quickly learned that in a big Italian family, you were never alone. There was always an aunt or uncle in the kitchen sipping a quick espresso at our king size wooden table. If that table could talk, you'd hear juicy gossip, praises for my older sister Lina, or a comment or two about my weight. Because of this I learned to avoid the spotlight, a hard task, especially among three siblings. There were countless occasions for us to squabble, fight, and eat. Many took place around that same wooden table. In fact, three things defined my youth: cakes, chips, and communions. In a big family, the spotlight was more of a high beam, and I was the deer caught between them. Headaches and all, I wouldn't trade my brothers and sister for the world. After all, this was my world, my life, and my family, and it is to them that I owe all my bumps, scrapes, and near death adventures. In every nook and cranny of the house there is a piece of history; add a story and season to taste. I didn't like my house, but I loved the candles, Doritos, and white dresses. I don't think any of my brothers or sister really liked the house either. The only room that made any sense to me was the kitchen.

As Italians, the kitchen was and still is the heart of the house and our lives. It seems like yesterday when I pulled up a chair to watch my mom prepare ravioli for the first time. The lure was inescapable in all of my innocence. It was just a matter of time before I turned in my sandbox and shovel for pasta and pots, but not before I planted the seeds of imagination. The kitchen became my stage, a place where magical characters came to life, and real ones disappeared. The smells would send me into a sensual trance. I remember when I was six; my mother had a terrible headache and was complaining to my father about how bad she felt. Instead of being worried, my immediate concern was if we would make ravioli first. My mom always laughs when she tells this story. Rather, my reaction constitutes a reminiscent smile. It's a pre-programmed recollection for the age-old statement, "You must always remember your roots." I love to cook because it brings family and friends together with all the good times and laughter you can associate with a dish. I remember Sunday lunches full of fond memories, heated conversations, great laughs, and of course, delicious food like lasagna, ravioli, or cannelloni, to mention a few. My mom is a great Italian cook and a major influence in my love for food.

My love for food continued into my teens, where I spent hours lost in front of the television with my late brother Frank. While most teens were out shopping or at home on the phone, we watched cooking shows. A strange pastime for some, but a comfort for us, as it distracted us from unraveling innocence. Although most shows were boring, at a time when reality shows were not at their peak, I stayed focused. The entertaining likes of Emeril Lagasse, Bobby Flay, Christine Cushing, and Jamie Oliver, to mention a few, were a little after our teen era. This was my school of hard knocks and I graduated at the top of my class. I not only learned the art of cooking, but also had a return ticket to travel the world at the touch of a button. Cooking was an entertaining escape; rare moments of confidence, no insecurities, and a place to hide out. The freedom to create and my fascination with different cultures eventually steered me away from Italy, away from my roots. My travels would take me to far and exotic places.

I began cooking Chinese, Spanish, and Indian foods, especially on days my mom prepared dishes I didn't like. The advantage of growing up in an Italian home is the access to two kitchens. My older brother and I would get together and create amazing dishes amidst debates and screams. Some days we got adventurous and had both kitchens going. Who needs a stair climber when you can cook between the basement and upstairs kitchens! Our big problem was that we both wanted to be in charge, but someone had to be the gofer. We had to somehow convince my older sister Lina and younger brother Vito to be involved. Lina did more taste testing than helping. Lina didn't and still doesn't enjoy cooking, but she did and still supports me unconditionally. I owe my drive to continue this book to Lina and Vito. I owe my passion and love for exotic cuisine to my late brother, who ignited my excitement about making all these new and fabulous dishes. We lost my older brother Frank on November 17, 2001. I lost a piece of myself that day, and all our lives changed forever. We refer to him as our angel, and he is one of my inspirations for writing this book. Knowing him was the best gift he could have ever given me. Without my co-chef, it was going to be difficult to keep up with my exotic adventures. Since a trip to China, Europe, and India were not possible at that the time, my passion for the exotic was focused on Jamaica.

Jamaica captivated me. It's a feeling I can't explain. You can see it in the faces of the people, and you feel and experience it through their beauty, music, food, and gorgeous island. It's a feeling of being comfortable, not knowing exactly why, but knowing that you are. Like God, I can't prove he exists, but I know that he does, and I see it in the beauty around me. When I visited the Island for the first time, the moment I bit into a festival, my communion with Jamaica was solidified. Yet even with my spiritual awakening and bright white dress, I was blinded by the obvious. It's funny, I spent two weeks on the Island, and every morning in the buffet they had Ackee and salt fish. But every day I would pass on them for the more traditional North American breakfast dishes. It was my fix for the familiar. On the very last day, as I walked past the Ackee and salt fish, I overheard a conversation. Couples went on about how good the dish was. Being the curious person that I am, I tried the Ackee and salt fish with fried dumpling, and I was in heaven. I loved it so much and was so angry with myself for not trying it sooner. This is so unlike me, because I like trying everything at least once. I suppose nothing truly happens before its time. This is when my love affair with Jamaican food started. Since my first trip, I've been back to Jamaica several times; in fact, I married a wonderful man who happens to be Jamaican, and love has become paradise.

My quest to be a great Jamaican cook started the day I met Nanny (Roslyn Rocto), on my second trip to the Island. My husband's now late grandmother had a love for Jamaica and cooking that soared high above the clouds. We would sit and talk under the shade of the trees in her front yard. The cool breeze and her tall stories were reminiscent of a time long ago. I remember her saying to me how important it was to be a good Jamaican cook because her grandson loved Jamaican food. She also said, "Always cook with your heart and let your fingers do the work." She constantly reminded me how important family is. It was that conversation that made me feel so at home and comfortable with her, because we share the same idealism toward food and family. In fact, I loved being in Jamaica so much and loved the food even more, that this is when I came up with the idea to write the book back in 1998.

Many people associate Jamaican cuisine with curry and jerk. While both are very popular and delicious, there is so much more. It's about an exciting culture that is as diverse as it's food; in fact, Jamaica's motto is "out of many people, one." You will see the many influences in the food from the many cultures that lived and still live in Jamaica, such as Indian, African, Asian, and European. All the recipes are so easy to prepare; some do require time, but it is well worth it. Many, if not all, will become part of the meals that you prepare for many years to come.

This book represents my love and passion for Jamaica and its food. This is about family and friends and all the good times around the dinner table. This is my contribution to show the world Jamaica's unique culture, and it's a legacy for my son, so that he too can be proud of his Jamaican background. It's a cookbook filled with love and great cooking. It was an idea that started many years ago, and with my many inspirations, which include Nanny, I completed the book, and as my husband said, "It's about time." This book is about old Jamaica meets new Jamaica meets me. I have included all the traditional recipes and some more contemporary Jamaican inspired recipes. Each recipe uses all the ingredients indigenous to the island. I want this book to be for the Jamaicans that came to North America and lost track of their food, and of course, for the world to discover the wonderful world of Jamaican cooking. The photos within are of my personal experiences, so you are seeing Jamaica and her foods through my eyes. This is truly what you see is what you get, and it's a book with a big heart. I'm not a professional chef; I'm just a woman who loves to cook and needs to show the everyday cook that you don't need a picture perfect meal for it to be great. I'm no Martha Stewart, but the recipes speak for themselves. "One love, one heart, come to Jamaica and feel all right."

GLOSSARY

The list of ingredients may seem long for some of the recipes; however, don't let that deter you. Most of the ingredients are roughly chopped, therefore requiring little time. You will also notice that most of the recipes have the same seasoning (ingredients), which make it easier for you to follow and prepare. I have included many grilled recipes that are easy to prepare and are healthy. I use olive oil for most of my dishes; however, with some of the recipes, you must use a vegetable oil. Most Jamaicans prepare their meals over the stovetop, which includes roasts of many kinds. I have opted for the oven, because as we know, in North America, it's all about time. Jamaica to me is Blue Mountain coffee, **Appleton Jamaica Rum**, amazing food, reggae, white sand beaches, family and friends. What more could anyone want? Allow me to tempt your palate and transport your taste buds to paradise, where the sun shines and the pulsing beat of the Island continues into the night. "No worries, Mon!"

All of the ingredients in my book can easily be found in any grocery store and/or East Indian stores throughout North America.

ACKEE–Jamaica's national fruit, used as a vegetable that tastes like one too; resembles scrambled eggs. Ackee was brought over from Africa, most likely with the arrival of the slaves. It is the fruit of an evergreen tree; Ackee is grown in abundance in Jamaica. When ripe, it splits in three and the yellowish edible portion is the part that is cooked. It is packaged in cans and imported and can now be found throughout North America; this is cooked with salt fish to make Jamaica's national dish. (brand, **Grace Products**)

ALLSPICE–Jamaicans refer to this as pimento. This is the dried unripe berry of a tree that is indigenous to Jamaica and is a very important spice. This is an important part of the seasoning for jerk sauce and many other dishes. You can buy ground or the allspice berry (you can grind).

AVACODO–To Jamaicans it's known as pear, sold in most grocery stores in North America. Jamaicans eat this on a sandwich on hardough bread.

BANANA–Both green and ripe are very important to Jamaican cuisine. Green bananas are not to be eaten raw; they are to be boiled.

BREADFRUIT–It's a large green fruit and has a bumpy skin. It can be peeled and fried, or cooked, just like a potato. It can also be roasted in the skin and then peeled. It's served as a starchy vegetable, like any of the root vegetables, and is great with ackee and salt fish. This is available canned or fresh in West Indian stores (brand, **Grace Products**).

BROWNING–This product is used to help darken meat, cakes, and buns (brand, **Grace Products**).

CALABAZA, West Indian PUMPKIN–Not to be confused with the North American pumpkin, the Caribbean is round or oval and its skin color is greenish or yellow with some white. It is most commonly used in soups, and its best substitute would be the butternut squash.

CALLALOO–A green leafy vegetable grown in Jamaica and is part of the Chinese spinach family. It is used in soups or served as a vegetable dish. It is available canned in West Indian stores (brand, **Grace Products**). You can substitute it with spinach.

CASSAVA–A large vegetable that has a tough brown skin with a very firm white flesh; Jamaicans use this to make bammy, which is served with fried fish. You can buy ready-to-eat bammy in most West Indian stores.

CHAYOTE SQUASH–A pale green squash shaped like a pear used in soups; Jamaicans refer to it as cho cho.

CILANTRO- Referred to as coriander or Chinese parsley. It's an herb with wide delicate green leaves and has a pungent flavor. Easily confused with flat-leaf parsley in appearance, so be sure to smell carefully.

CHO CHO (COCO)–An edible starchy root that tastes similar to a potato and Dasheen. Best when boiled.

COCONUT MILK–I use the canned coconut milk and it works just fine. To make your own coconut milk, you cut the meat from a coconut into small pieces and blend in a food processor; then add plain warm water until liquefied, put through a strainer several times, squeezing out all of the pulp.

CURRY–This is a very important spice for Jamaicans, as they love to eat and prepare many curry dishes, and in particular, curry chicken and curry goat. Jamaican curry (Caribbean curry) is very different than East Indian curry, as they do not add as many ingredients. When you are preparing Jamaican dishes, please try to find a good Caribbean curry, preferably Jamaican (brand, **Grace Product**). I make my own and it happens to be one of the best I've tasted; this was Nanny's recipe, which one day I hope to sell to major stores around the world.

DASHEEN–Also known as taro, tania and eddo. Dasheen is a starchy root vegetable that is usually served boiled, but regular potatoes can often be used as a substitute in recipes calling for dasheen.

EDDOE–They are small and round with a brown skin and have a hairy appearance; the flesh is cut into cubes for soups or served with meat or fish dishes.

ESCOVITCH–The Spanish word for pickled, usually for fresh fish that is fried; it consists of vinegar, spices, hot pepper and oil.

JAMAICAN SWEET POTATO–Also called boniata and batata. Unlike the regular sweet potato, the skin has a dark pink, purple to burgundy color and the flesh is a creamy yellow. It has a taste of roasted chestnuts and has a fluffier texture. They should be stored at room temperature and used immediately. Best when boiled.

LIMES–Caribbean limes have light yellow skins when ripe; however, they are picked green, because they go bad very quickly when ripe. Limes are one of the most used ingredients in Jamaican cooking. They are used in sauces, marinades, and drinks. Limes are used in savory and sweet dishes to add pizzazz.

MANGO–This fruit actually is native to India; it has come to be known as "the fruit of the tropics." Mangos are used in a variety of ways in Jamaica. They are used for sauces, condiments, desserts, and drinks.

NUTMEG–This spice has a spicy sweet flavor and is used in cakes, puddings, and drinks. Jamaicans will not use ground nutmeg spice, insisting on grating it themselves.

OKRA—This finger-like shaped vegetable is green and approximately four inches long; it is used in soups, the most popular being the pepperpot soup.

PAPAYA—A sweet fruit used in sauces, condiments, beverages, and ice cream, or eaten plain, as you would any other fruit. Do not eat the seeds in the middle; it resembles a melon, and as you would with a melon, remove seeds and peel. Fresh papayas are widely available in most grocery stores.

PEAS—Are actually red kidney beans and are used in Jamaica's most popular rice dish (Rice and Peas) and soup (Red Pea Soup); however, pigeon peas can also be used.

PLANTAIN—A member of the banana family, but unlike a banana, you cannot eat it raw. A ripe plantain will turn a yellowish color and may have many black spots. The plantain is at it's sweetest when it is fully black. Plantains are best when fried, boiled, grilled, or baked. Plantains are available in most grocery stores and in West Indian stores.

SALT FISH—In North America it's referred to as salt cod and is very important to Jamaican cuisine; after all, Ackee and salt fish is Jamaica's national dish. Many dishes are made with salt fish, like salt fish balls, salt fish fritters, and seasoned rice, to mention a few. Salt fish is very salty and should be soaked overnight; however, if you don't have the time, you can remove the salt by boiling in water several times, removing the water after each boil. Once it's been cooked, drain and flake with a fork.

SCALLION—North Americans refer to them as spring onions, and again, they are very popular in many Jamaican dishes.

SCOTCH BONNET PEPPERS—A fiery hot pepper, ranging in color from yellow to orange to red, and is probably the most popular pepper for Jamaicans. It also has a fruitiness that makes this pepper, in my opinion, the best tasting. Nonetheless, you can substitute with any hot pepper you like. **NOTE**: You can leave pepper out completely in any of my recipes. They still work out fine, even with jerk. Believe me; I've made it many times without the pepper; use more ginger.

SORREL—Brought from India, this unusual plant was introduced to Jamaica by the British. Sorrel always blooms in December, and this is when the "red flower" becomes Jamaica's traditional holiday beverage.

STAR FRUIT—This is a star shaped fruit with an acidy-sweet taste, used in desserts or as a garnish.

SOYA SAUCE—This condiment is very important in many Jamaican dishes, considering the very large Asian population. Most Jamaicans I know use the **dark Soya sauce with mushroom flavor.** I find it really adds good flavor to many of the dishes.

THYME—The most popular Jamaican herb it just happens to work well with just about everything, including meat, fish, vegetables, and poultry. It is used in soups, stew, barbeques, and sauces.

YAMS—Can either have a yellow or white flesh and has a nutty flavor; usually found in soups, and accompanies many dishes in this book.

Also very important to Jamaican cooking and the recipes in this book are **GARLIC, GINGER, ONION, HOISIN SAUCE, SESAME OIL, RUM, AND CRUSHED RED PEPPER SAUCE.**

LET'S START COOKIN, MON! ♥

CONDIMENTS (SAUCES)

The sauces and toppings in this section are good with just about any meat or fish dish. Bring your taste to a new level and experience the marrying of fruits with savory foods that work so well together. I'm sure that all of these sauces will be used to accompany many of the dishes in the book, like coconut shrimp with roasted red pepper sauce, grilled shrimp with papaya mint sauce, or grilled steak served with garlic and thyme sauce, just to mention a few. Hot pepper is very important in Jamaican cuisine, and if you like it hot, then you have to try the mango and papaya chutney or the tomato chutney. One heart, one love, all in one stomach; whatever the saying, cook Jamaican and feel all right.

JAMAICA IS LUSH, GREEN, AND BEAUTIFUL A PERFECT PLACE TO TAKE A WALK IN THE MIDDLE OF THE AFTERNOON WHICH IS ALSO A GOOD WAY TO WORK OFF SOME OF THE EXTRA CALORIES.

PAPAYA MINT SASLA

This is so refreshing and really works well with grilled dishes. Everyone who has tried it loves it. ♥

- 2 medium papayas (small dice - cubed)
- 2 tablespoons each of **fresh mint, and oil (vegetable or olive)**
- 2 tablespoons of fresh lime juice
- salt and black pepper to taste

COOKING AND PREPARATION INSTRUCTIONS

STEP 1.   In a bowl add the papaya, fresh mint, lime juice, oil and salt and pepper. Mix until well combine and refrigerate until ready to use. Best results let sit and combine for 15 minutes.

Serve with any grilled dish; grilled shrimp pg 27 or grilled steak pg 75 just to mention a few.

TOMATO CHUTNEY

- 2 cups of tomatoes- peeled and chopped
- ½ cup of vinegar
- 1 tablespoon of lime juice
- 1 clove of garlic (minced)
- 1 small onion (finely chopped)
- 1 tablespoon of fresh ginger (finely chopped)
- 2 tablespoons of hot sauce (**Grace Product** or any brand)
- 1 cup of water
- salt and black pepper to taste

COOKING AND PREPARATION INSTRUCTIONS

STEP 1.   In a small pot add all the ingredients, cook on medium heat for 45–60 minutes until thickened. Easy to double.

Serve with seasoned meatballs pg 23, curry fish cakes pg 32, breaded fish fillets pg 127, and more.

TOMATO AND PEPPER RELISH

- 2 medium tomatoes (finely diced)
- 1 green pepper (finely diced)
- 1 small red onion (finely diced)
- 1/3 cup of olive oil
- 2 tablespoons each of fresh **mint or cilantro**, **lime juice**, **white vinegar,** and **hot sauce** (any brand)

COOKING AND PREPARATION INSTRUCTIONS

STEP 1.   Combine all the ingredients; mix well and refrigerate until ready to use.

Serve with grilled steak pg 74, breaded fish fillets pg 127, grilled salmon pg 131, and more.

MANGO SALSA

This is not only very refreshing, but it is low in fat and a great accompaniment to so many dishes. ♥

- 2 ripe firm mangos, peeled (cut into small cubes) (not over ripe mango's)
- 1 red pepper (cut into small cubes)
- ½ of a green pepper (cut into small cubes)
- 1/3 cup of a red onion (cut into small cubes)
- ¼ cup of oil (your choice)
- 2 tablespoons of fresh mint (finely chopped)
- 3 tablespoons of fresh lime juice
- salt and black pepper to taste
- 1 scotch bonnet pepper (finely chopped) **(optional)**

COOKING AND PREPARATION INSTRUCTIONS

STEP 1.   In a bowl combine all ingredients together; mix well and refrigerate until ready to use.

Serve with many dishes, such as grilled meats and seafood; for example, grilled boneless pork roast (pg 92), jerk chicken or pork pg 109, grilled salmon pg 131, and the list goes on.

AVOCADO AND TOMATO SALSA

This is a quick and refreshing topping for many grilled meat and fish dishes. This is pictured on pg 83. ♥

- 2 avocado's, peeled (cut into small cubes)
- 2 tomatoes (cut into small cubes)
- 1/3 cup of red onion (cut into small cubes)
- 4 tablespoons of fresh lime juice
- 1/3 cups of oil (your choice)
- 2 teaspoons of hot sauce (**Grace Product** or any brand) **(optional)**
- 2 tablespoon's of fresh mint (finely chopped)
- 4 tablespoons of fresh cilantro (finely chopped) (use as much as you like)
- salt and black pepper

COOKING AND PREPARATION INSTRUCTIONS

STEP 1.   In a bowl combine all ingredients together; mix well and refrigerate until ready to use. Easy to double.

This is a fabulous topping for special hut burgers pg 77, grilled salmon pg 131 and more. Great with pita bread and corn chips.

ROASTED RED PEPPER SAUCE

- ½ cup of plain yogurt
- 1 cup of light cream cheese
- 2 tablespoons of oil (your choice)
- 1 roasted pepper (skin and seeds removed and chopped)
- 1 small clove of garlic
- 3 tablespoon's of fresh lime juice
- 2 teaspoons of fresh thyme
- salt and black pepper to taste

COOKING AND PREPARATION INSTRUCTIONS

STEP 1.   Combine all ingredients in a blender and blend until a creamy sauce is achieved. Refrigerate until ready to use. Serve with coconut shrimp pg 36 or as a dip with crackers.

CREAMY MINT AND THYME SAUCE

- 1 cup of plain yogurt
- 1 cup of light cream cheese
- 4 tablespoons of oil (your choice)
- 2 small cloves of garlic
- 2 teaspoons of fresh thyme
- 2 tablespoons of fresh mint (roughly chopped)
- salt and black pepper to taste

COOKING AND PREPARATION INSTRUCTIONS
STEP 1.   Combine all ingredients in a blender and blend until a creamy sauce is achieved. Refrigerate until ready to use. This is great with broiled shrimp and scallops pg 29 barbequed chicken pg 102, and many fried dishes, or as a dip for crackers and vegetables.

FRESH CITRUS SAUCE

- 1/3 cup of each of oil and mayonnaise
- 2 tablespoons of vinegar
- 2 small cloves of garlic minced
- 2 tablespoons of fresh mint (chopped)
- 1 teaspoon of Dijon mustard
- 1 tablespoon each of lime and lemon zest
- 2 tablespoons of lemon and lime juice
- ¼ of pain yogurt
- salt and black pepper to taste

COOKING AND PREPARATION INSTRUCTIONS
STEP 1.   Combine all ingredients in a blender and blend until a really creamy sauce is achieved. Refrigerate until ready to use. Great with coconut shrimp, pg 36 broiled shrimp and scallops pg 29, breaded fish fillets pg 126, curry fish cakes pg 33, and salt fish fritters pg 34.

MANGO AND PAPAYA CHUTNEY

This is traditional served with curry dishes; however, it is great with any meat, chicken, or fish dish. This is pictured on pg 33. **SUBSTITUTE MANGOS AND PAPAYAS** with pineapple. ♥

- ➤ 1 cup of partially ripe or ripe mangos (diced)
- ➤ ½ cup of partially ripe or ripe papayas (diced)
- ➤ ½ cup of sugar
- ➤ 1½ teaspoons of fresh ginger (finely chopped)
- ➤ 1 clove of garlic (minced)
- ➤ ½ cup of vinegar
- ➤ 1 onion (finely chopped)
- ➤ 1½ teaspoons of salt
- ➤ 1 large green pepper (chopped into cubes)
- ➤ 1 scotch bonnet pepper (finely chopped)
- ➤ 1¼ cups of water

COOKING AND PREPARATION INSTRUCTIONS

STEP 1.   Combine all ingredients in a saucepan and simmer, stirring constantly for 60 minutes.

STEP 2.   Remove from heat, stir, and pour into a glass jar or Tupperware container; store in fridge for later use. Can be kept in the refrigerator for up to a week.

FRESH GARLIC AND THMYE SAUCE

Although this is not quite Jamaican—in fact, this is a quick version of Greek Tzatziki sauce—I have incorporated many Jamaican spices such as thyme and allspice, which gives new meaning to delicious. ♥

- ➤ 1½ cups of plain yogurt
- ➤ 1 teaspoon of allspice
- ➤ 2 tablespoons of mint (finely chopped)
- ➤ 1–2 teaspoons of fresh thyme (finely chopped)
- ➤ 4–5 cloves of garlic (minced)
- ➤ 2 tablespoons of olive oil (your choice)
- ➤ 2 teaspoons of white vinegar
- ➤ 1 tablespoon of fresh lime juice
- ➤ salt and black pepper to taste

COOKING AND PREPARATION INSTRUCTIONS

STEP 1.   In a bowl add all ingredients; mix well. Cover and refrigerate for 2 hours, or overnight for best results. If you want the sauce to be thicker place yogurt in a sieve in cheesecloth over a bowl for 4 to 8 hours in the fridge. The yogurt will be thick and creamy. Place the yogurt in a bowl and then add the ingredients; mix until combined.

Great with any grilled dishes, such as steak pg 74, roast beef pg 88, Spiced Leg of Lamb pg 94, and the list goes on. This is also great as a salad dressing.

APPETIZERS AND SIDES (GOODIES)

The appetizers in my book are a collection of traditional and not so traditional dishes. The majority I've gathered are from family and friends; however, some are my interpretations of goodies I experienced on the Island. I'm sure you may be familiar with at least one; however, you will enjoy all.

A Jamaican cookbook without BEEF PATTIES would be unwise, even sacrilegious. These tasty treats are as much a part of Jamaica as its rum and reggae. They are as Jamaican as pizza is Italian. A little complicated to tackle, but David didn't bring down Goliath without trying. Don't be afraid of the long list of ingredients, because they are so easy to prepare, not to mention delicious. I have served them to many people, including non-lovers, who now swear by them. I have included side dishes as well, such as festival and roti, the Jamaican versions of bread. So try the grilled shrimp with papaya mint sauce or the more traditional escovitched fish. I believe I have recipes that will satisfy everyone's taste buds; all you have to do is give them a try. Note, anytime I mention milk in my recipes you can use, whole milk, low fat, skim, 1% and 2 % however the fatter the milk the better the end result.

JAMAICA IS ALSO ABOUT ROMANCE. MY SISTER LINA AND HER HUSBAND VITO.

FESTIVAL

As the name suggests, these are a party for the taste buds and are sinfully delicious! This is a favorite of young and old alike, with one thought in mind, enjoying them on the beach as they are served in Jamaica. These babies are worth the extra 15 minutes on the treadmill. Live it up! This is pictured on pg 83. ♥

- 2 ½ cups of white (All purpose) flour
- 1 cup of cornmeal
- 2½ teaspoons of baking powder
- 3 teaspoons of salt
- 5-6 tablespoons of brown sugar
- 1½ cups of water
- ½ teaspoon of vanilla
- 1/3 cup of all-purpose + 3 tablespoons cornmeal to dip the festival before frying
- vegetable oil for frying

COOKING AND PREPARATION INSTRUCTIONS

STEP 1.   In a large bowl combine flour, baking powder, cornmeal, and salt; mix ingredients well.

STEP 2.   In another bowl add the water, sugar and vanilla and stir until sugar has dissolved. Slowly incorporate the water to the dry ingredients. With a spoon, mix until flour mixture and water come together to form a soft dough; then knead for a few minutes. If you find the dough too sticky, add more flour until you have soft, pliable dough.

STEP 3.   Cover with a damp cloth and let it rest for 1 hour in a dry place; do not refrigerate.

STEP 4.   Divide dough into approximately 10-15 portions; depending on your size preference. On a flat surface dust with flour (if needed) and roll each portion into a small log, or any other shape you like.

STEP 5.   Dip the festival in flour- cornmeal mixture. Turn the heat to medium. Place fry pan on heat and fill halfway with oil. Add the festivals to the hot oil and fry on each side until golden brown.

Tip: When shallow frying or deep frying-To test if the oil is hot enough use a wooden spoon and place the bottom of the handle into the oil and if it bubbles around it— it's ready. The oil should reach about 350 to 375 degree F when deep frying— use a candy thermometer.

This is traditionally served with Oxtail pg 76 or Jerk Chicken/Pork pg 109; however, it's great on its own or with just about any Jamaican dish.

ROTI

This was taught to me by my mother-in-law, who was taught by her mother-in-law, Nanny (who in my opinion made the best roti in Jamaica). This flat bread is not only easy to make, but is also a family classic. On its own it may not be a mouthwatering delight, but wrapped around morsels of chicken or goat and dipped in curry sauce, you have a little piece of heaven. Roti is a traditional side dish to most East Indian meals, but in Jamaica it has become an integral partner to all curry dishes. This is an example of art imitating life, or in this case, traditional island food imitating Jamaican culture. I suppose with the maiden name of Roti, I was destined to also be an integral part of Jamaican culture and cuisine. This is pictured on pg 79. ♥

- 4 cups of white (All purpose) flour sifted Atta Flour sold in most grocery stores
- 2½ teaspoons of salt (or to your taste)
- 1 teaspoon of baking powder
- 4 tablespoons of vegetable oil
- 1 teaspoon of honey
- 1½–2 cups of lukewarm water (start with 1½ cups) not hot but not cold in the middle!
- vegetable oil for frying + 1/3 cup of vegetable oil for brushing on the roti

COOKING AND PREPARATION INSTRUCTIONS

STEP 1. In a large bowl add the flour, salt, baking powder set aside.

STEP 2. In another large bowl add the water, oil, and honey stir. Add water mixture to the flour and mix until you form a soft dough; with your hands, knead for 8- 10 minutes. Dough should be pliable and soft. Return dough to bowl and let dough rest for 1 hour covered with a damp cloth in a warm place.

STEP 3. Divide dough into approximately 8 small portions and form into balls. On a flat surface dust with some flour (if needed) and roll out each portion into a thin, flat round shape (8–10-inch circles).

STEP 4. Turn the heat to medium. Place a flat pan, griddle, tawa, or a regular fry pan on the heat and add oil. When pan becomes hot place one roti at a time and cook on medium heat until both sides of the roti have brown flecks/bubbles on the surface.

STEP 5. Remove and place on a plate; with a clean kitchen cloth cover the roti and press firmly down with your hands. Keep the kitchen cloth over the roti. Keep warm. Makes 8 – 10 small roti's.

Note: You can also combine 2 cups of atta flour and 2 cups of white all purpose flour. The roti should be rolled out very thin, but don't be discouraged if you can't get them really thin; you will get better with time. Thick or thin, they will still taste good. The longer you knead the better the end result. Cover left over roti's in foil. To reheat roti place on a microwavable plate and cover with a dampen paper towel and microwave for 50 seconds.

These are typically served with any curry dish, such a curry goat, chicken, beef, fish, and seafood.

BOILED DUMPLINGS

Boiled dumplings are not usually eaten on their own; they are best when enjoyed with dishes such as Ackee and Salt Fish, Red Pea Soup, and Rundown, just to mention a few. This is pictured on pg 82. ♥

- ➤ 3 cups of white (All-purpose) flour
- ➤ salt to taste
- ➤ water (enough to combine approx. 1¼ cups)

COOKING AND PREPARATION INSTRUCTIONS

STEP 1.   In a large bowl add the flour and salt mix well. Add the **water slowly** until mixture comes together. If it feels too sticky, add more flour; if it feels too dry, add more water. Knead for a 5 minutes and let stand (rest) for 10 minutes, and then shape into discs (saucer shape 2-inch circles).

STEP 2.   In a medium pot fill water enough to cover dumplings. Turn heat to medium.

STEP 3.   Place pot on heat and bring to a boil; add the dumplings and stir. Cook dumplings on medium heat for 15 minutes, until the dumplings float to the top. Stir dumplings occasionally to avoid sticking to pot. Drain and keep warm. Makes about 10-12 dumplings.

Dumplings for soups or stews are made long and thin referred to as spinners. With the palms of your hands facing each other, roll a piece of dough between them until you form a thin log about 3-4 inches long.

FRIED DUMPLINGS

What can I say ... these are probably on an Atkins' top 10 worst things to eat list, but boy are they delicious. This is pictured on pg 79. Enjoy with pick up salt fish or ackee and salt fish ♥

- 3 cups of white (All-purpose) flour
- salt to taste
- 3 teaspoons of baking powder
- water (enough to combine approx. 1¼ cups)
- oil for frying

COOKING AND PREPARATION INSTRUCTIONS

STEP 1.   In a large bowl add the flour, salt, and baking powder; mix well. Add water slowly until mixture comes together. If it feels too sticky, add more flour, and if it feels too dry, add more water. Knead for 5 minutes and let stand (rest) for 10 minutes, and then shape into discs. Turn the heat to medium.

STEP 2.   Place fry pan on heat and fill halfway with oil. Add the dumplings to the hot oil and fry on each side until golden brown. Makes about 12.

Tip: When shallow frying or deep frying-To test if the oil is hot enough use a wooden spoon and place the bottom of the handle into the oil and if it bubbles around it— it's ready. The oil should reach about 350 to 375 degree F when deep frying— use a candy thermometer.

SEASONED MEATBALLS

Don't let the long list of ingredients scare you off. This is really easy and great for buffets as well as appetizers. Looking to give a new spicy life to meatballs? Then look no further, for you have found it. This is pictured on pg 81. ♥

- ➢ 1 pound of ground beef
- ➢ salt and black pepper to taste
- ➢ 1½ cups of breadcrumbs
- ➢ 1 teaspoon of allspice
- ➢ ½ teaspoon of baking powder **(optional)**
- ➢ 4 cloves of garlic (minced)
- ➢ 2 stalks of scallions (finely chopped)
- ➢ 1 tablespoon of fresh thyme (finely chopped) (if using dried thyme use 1 teaspoon)
- ➢ 2 teaspoons of fresh ginger (finely chopped)
- ➢ 1 green pepper (finely chopped)
- ➢ 2 teaspoons of soya sauce
- ➢ 2 tablespoon each of fresh mint or cilantro (finely chopped)
- ➢ 1 scotch bonnet pepper (finely chopped) **(optional)**
- ➢ ½ cup of water
- ➢ 1 large egg
- ➢ vegetable oil for frying or baking (you can use olive oil, if you choose to bake)

COOKING AND PREPARATION INSTRUCTIONS

STEP 1. In a large bowl combine all ingredients, mix well, and form round shapes that are slightly flattened, as it makes for easy frying. (You can also shape them like the salt fish balls (pg 32), which is also easy for frying.) You can either fry or bake.

IF FRYING- Turn heat to medium. Place the fry pan to the heat and add oil your choice (1/3 cup). Add the meatballs to the hot oil and fry on both sides until golden and fully cooked (about 10–15 minutes).

IF BAKING- Grease pan with your choice of oil and bake for about 10–15 minutes in a 350 degree oven, turning once halfway during cooking. To achieve a nice golden color, brush the meat with a little oil before baking.

TIP- If the mixture is too dry, add water; if too wet, add breadcrumbs. When forming patties, have some water or oil handy; this will help you in forming the balls.

To serve, place meatballs on toothpicks or wooden skewers. Serve with your favorite sauce. A great sauce would be the tomato chutney pg 14, or mango and papaya chutney pg 17.

This makes about 25–30 meatballs.

SUBSTITUTE BEEF with ground pork, chicken, turkey, or shrimp.

BEEF PATTY

This is the Jamaican version of the English meat pie. I believe it's better; and trust me, you will love them too. If you make these for your family and friends, they will be so impressed, and you don't even have to tell them how easy they were to prepare. This is one of the most recognizable foods of the Caribbean. Remember, this is my take, so I hope I have done Jamaican patties justice; I think I have. This is a great after school snack for your kids to enjoy, plus they freeze well. If it were up to my son, I would have to prepare them every day. This is a combination of recipes from several family members and friends. This is pictured on page 81. ♥

What to know- The following two spices can be used in the dough for coloring purposes only. You can omit either spice; however, patties are known for their color. Both spices can be found in most major grocery stores, East Indian stores, or Latin markets.

Turmeric – This spice is an important part of making most curry powder; it is what gives the distinctive color that curry is known for. It tastes like ginger or mustard, at least to me it does. This spice may stain hands and clothes; however, it's usually temporary. I usually add ¼ teaspoon of paprika with the 1 teaspoon of turmeric when making the patty shells.

Annatto - Is sometimes referred to as a "poor man's saffron"; this is a common spice found in Caribbean and South American cooking. The flavor can be described as earthy, somewhat peppery, and sweet. This spice may stain hands and clothes; however, it's usually temporary.

PATTY SHELLS

- ➢ 4 cups of white (All- purpose) flour
- ➢ 2½ teaspoons of salt (or to your taste)
- ➢ 1 teaspoon of ground turmeric powder or annatto powder
- ➢ 1 cup of cold unsalted butter (Cubed)
- ➢ ½ cup of cold unsalted margarine or shortening
- ➢ 1 large egg
- ➢ 1 tablespoon of cider vinegar or white vinegar
- ➢ cold ice water

DIRECTIONS FOR PASTRY

STEP 1. In a large bowl add the flour, salt, and turmeric powder and mix well. Add the margarine or shortening and butter. Cut butter and margarine with a knife, and then use your hands or pastry blender until the mixture resembles oatmeal (crumbly). Form a well in the center.

STEP 2. In a measuring cup (1 cup) add one beaten egg, vinegar, and then add enough water to bring the ingredients to a full cup.

STEP 3. Add ½ cup of the egg mixture to the center of the dough mixture, stir with a fork, and add remaining liquid slowly until mixture comes together.

STEP 4. Form dough into a ball, flatten slightly, wrap in a clean kitchen cloth or plastic wrap, and refrigerate for 1–2 hours.

STEP 5. Remove from fridge and divide dough into pieces; roll on a lightly floured surface into the size of a dessert plate; should be rolled out thin, about 1/8 inch. You can make them as large or as small as you like. Patty shells should be easy to roll out; try not to overwork the dough too much. If the dough feels wet and sticky add more flour to the dough when rolling out.

STEP 6. Fill (as detailed below) and bake.

Note- For Patty shell you can use only margarine (1½ cups), or you can use only shortening (1½ cups), or 1 cup of shortening and ½ cup of margarine. All variations will work. For a really flake dough make sure butter is really cold and also the water.

FILLING

- ➢ 1 pound of ground beef
- ➢ 3 tablespoons of oil (your choice)
- ➢ 2 small stalks of scallions (finely chopped)
- ➢ 5 cloves of garlic (minced)
- ➢ 1 green pepper (finely chopped)
- ➢ 1 medium onion (finely chopped)
- ➢ 1–2 teaspoons of ginger (finely chopped)
- ➢ 2–3 tablespoons of hot pepper sauce (any kind)
- ➢ 3 teaspoons of fresh thyme (finely chopped)
- ➢ 3 tablespoons of soya sauce (dark, preferably mushroom flavor)
- ➢ 1½–2½ teaspoons of curry powder
- ➢ 2 teaspoons of allspice and ground thyme
- ➢ salt and black pepper to taste
- ➢ ¾ cups of water
- ➢ ½ cup of breadcrumbs

COOKING AND PREPARATION INSTRUCTIONS FOR FILLING

STEP 1. In a bowl add the breadcrumbs and water and mix well. Set aside until mixture thickens. You will need this for step 4.

STEP 2. Turn heat to medium. Place pot or frying pan on heat and add oil. Add the scallions, garlic, green pepper, onion, ginger, and scotch bonnet to the hot oil and fry until vegetables are soft about 5–10 minutes.

STEP 3. Add ground beef, and then add crushed fresh thyme, curry powder, allspice, ground thyme and black pepper and continue on medium heat. Cook until beef is no longer pink, stirring frequently to avoid sticking to the pan. Add soya sauce and mix well. Add salt and taste for seasonings.

STEP 4. Add breadcrumb mixture to meat mixture; continue to cook and stir constantly for 5–10 minutes until mixture is thick. Taste for seasonings and adjust if needed. Cool mixture.

STEP 5. In the center of each patty shell, add 1½-2 tablespoons of the mixture; brush along the edges with water or egg wash, fold into a half moon shape and press along the edges with a fork to help secure the patty. Poke a few holes on top. (Don't overfill patties or they will open slightly.) Bake in a 350 degree oven for 20–25 minutes, until golden.

This makes about 15 medium patties. Refrigerate leftovers and reheat in oven or microwave oven.

SUBSTITUTE BEEF with ground pork, chicken, turkey, or shrimp.

DEEP FRIED SQUID

I took the classic deep fried squid and jazzed it up with Jamaica spice. Is anyone in the mood for some reggae? ♥

- 2½ pounds of squid (cleaned, pat dried and cut into rings or strips)
- ¾ cup of white (All purpose) flour
- 2 teaspoons of allspice
- 1½ teaspoons of garlic powder
- ½ teaspoon of ground thyme
- 3 teaspoons of paprika
- ½ teaspoon of ground cayenne pepper **(optional)**
- salt and black pepper to taste

COOKING AND PREPARATION INSTRUCTIONS

STEP 1. Wash and clean squid, pat dry, and cut into 2–3-inch rings or strips.

STEP 2. Combine flour with the allspice, garlic powder, ground thyme, paprika, cayenne, salt and black pepper.

STEP 3. In a bowl with the squid, add the flour mixture and combine well. Shake off any access flour from the squid with a strainer or sieve. Turn the heat to medium.

STEP 4. Place fry pan or wok on heat and fill halfway with oil. Add the squid in batches into the hot oil; fry until golden brown, about 2–3 minutes. Remove and place on paper towels over a plate and sprinkle with more salt. Transfer to a serving plate or bowl and serve. Discard any left over flour.

Tip: When shallow frying or deep frying-To test if the oil is hot enough use a wooden spoon and place the bottom of the handle into the oil and if it bubbles around it— it's ready. The oil should reach about 350 to 375 degree F when deep frying— use a candy thermometer.

Try not to overcook squid, as it will become rubbery. Squid should be cooked either quickly or slow-cooked (stewed) to achieve a tender end product.

Serve immediately with lemon or lime.

Try this classic dish with the roasted red pepper sauce, creamy mint and thyme sauce pg 16, fresh garlic and thyme sauce pg 17, fresh citrus sauce pg 16, or spicy mayo sauce pg 127. This is also great with commercial tarter sauce.

GRILLED SHRIMP

This is a great appetizer. This dish was inspired by a dish I had in a restaurant in Jamaica. This is full of flavor that I am confident will impress everyone you serve them to. No worries, mon, this is quick and easy. This is pictured on page 81. ♥

- 3 tablespoons of fresh lime juice
- salt and black pepper to taste
- 1 teaspoon of allspice
- 2 tablespoons of soya sauce (preferably dark mushroom flavor)
- 4 cloves of garlic (minced)
- 1 tablespoon of fresh thyme (finely chopped) or 1 teaspoon of ground thyme
- 2 tablespoons of fresh mint or cilantro (finely chopped)
- 2 stalks of scallions (finely chopped)
- ¼ -1/3 cup of oil (your choice)
- 1 onion chopped into 1-inch cubes **(optional)**
- 2½ pounds of shrimp (remove shell and de-vein or leave in shell for more flavor)
- skewers (If using wooden skewers-soak skewers in water to avoid burning)

COOKING AND PREPARATION INSTRUCTIONS

STEP 1.   In a large bowl combine lime juice, salt, black pepper, allspice, soya sauce, garlic, thyme, mint, scallions, and oil; mix well. Add shrimps and onion to mixture and again mix well. Refrigerate for 1 hour.

STEP 2.   For every skewer, alternate shrimp, and onion (3–4 shrimp per skewer).

STEP 3.   Preheat barbeque to medium and make sure to grease the grill to avoid sticking.

STEP 4.   Grill the shrimps for 3–4 minutes per side on medium to high heat until shrimp turns pink and curls slightly. Top with the chopped fresh mint and cilantro.

Eat and enjoy!

Serve with papaya mint sauce, fresh citrus sauce pg 16, spicy mango sauce pg 93, mango salsa pg 15, or any of your favorite sauces.

Serves 4 people as an appetizer.

SPICY GRILLED GINGER SHRIMP

If you want to get your party going, this is a great way to start with a bang. This is my grilled version of peppered shrimp, with a twist or two, of course, *a/a* Mary style. ♥

- 3 pounds of large shrimp (wash and dry well and de-vein; for more flavor leave shell on)
- 3 tablespoons of fresh lime juice
- salt and black pepper
- 1½ tablespoons of paprika
- 2 stalks of scallions (finely chopped)
- 2 tablespoons of fresh ginger (finely chopped)
- 4 cloves of garlic (minced)
- 1 tablespoon of fresh thyme (finely chopped)
- 2 scotch bonnet peppers or any hot pepper (chopped) (you can add less)
- 1/3 cup of oil (your choice) (you can use less; ¼ would be okay)
- skewers (If using wooden skewers- soak skewers in water to avoid burning)

COOKING AND PREPARATION INSTRUCTIONS

STEP 1. In a large bowl add the lime juice, salt, black pepper, paprika, scallions, ginger, garlic, thyme, hot pepper, and oil; mix gently. Add shrimp to the mixture and again mix well; refrigerate for 1 hour.

STEP 2. Place 3 shrimps per skewer or place all the shrimp in a BBQ grill basket.

STEP 3. Preheat barbeque to medium and make sure to grease the grill to avoid sticking.

STEP 4. Grill the shrimps for 3–4 minutes per side or until the shrimps turns pink and curls slightly. Top with chopped mint or cilantro (optional)

Squeeze lime on shrimp, serve, and enjoy. Serve with the fresh citrus sauce pg 16, spicy mango sauce pg 93.

A NICE NEEDED BREAK FROM THE HUSTLE AND BUSTLE.

Serves 4 as an appetizer.

BROILED SHRIMP AND SCALLOPS

This is a really great way to start off a formal dinner party and is always a hit when I serve them. I had this in an Italian restaurant and thought this would be fabulous with Jamaican spices, and boy, was I right. That is the great thing about cooking; you can always try new things. ♥

- 1 pound of medium scallops (cleaned)
- 1 pound of medium shrimp (cleaned and shells removed)
- $\frac{3}{4}$ cup of unflavored breadcrumbs
- $\frac{3}{4}$ cup of oil (your choice)
- $\frac{1}{4}$ cup of fresh mint (finely chopped)
- 2 tablespoons of chopped cilantro **(optional)**
- 3 cloves of garlic (minced)
- 1 to 2 teaspoons of fresh ginger (finely chopped)
- 2 each teaspoon of allspice and ground thyme
- salt and black pepper to taste
- lime wedges
- 8 metal skewers

COOKING AND PREPARATION INSTRUCTIONS

STEP 1. Wash shrimp and scallops under cold water and pat dry. Season with salt and pepper.

STEP 2. In a large bowl combine breadcrumbs, oil, mint, cilantro, garlic, ginger, allspice, ground thyme salt, and black pepper.

STEP 3. Add shrimp and scallops to mixture, and mix until well coated. Refrigerate for 45 minutes to 1 hour.

STEP 4. Preheat broiler. Place shrimp and scallops alternately on metal skewers and press in more of the breadcrumb mixture. Place skewers on a greased cookie pan and broil for 4–7 minutes per side, until golden. You can bake in a 350 degree oven for about 10 minutes or until golden.

Sprinkle with more fresh chopped mint if desired.

Serve with lime. Here are a couple of great sauces that will complement this dish: the creamy mint and thyme sauce, mango salsa pg 15 or garlic and thyme sauce pg 17.

Serves 4 people.

ESCOVITCHED FISH

Auntie Wah, who lives in Spanish Town Jamaica, is the inspiration for this recipe; she is an incredible cook. This is usually served as a snack or finger food. The fish is commonly left whole; however, for this recipe I chose to have the fish in fillets. This is quick and easy. This method of marinating came from the Spanish and Portuguese. This is pictured on page 81. ❤

- 2½ pounds of medium to large fish fillets (red snapper, ocean perch, or rainbow trout)
- salt and black pepper to taste
- 6 tablespoons of white (All purpose) flour
- 1/3 cup of oil (your choice)
- 1½ cups of vinegar
- ½ cup of water
- 1 large onion (sliced thinly)
- 1 cup of carrots (sliced thinly)
- 1 whole scotch bonnet or your choice of hot pepper (chopped)
- 3 teaspoons of allspice
- juice of one lime

COOKING AND PREPARATION INSTRUCTIONS

STEP 1. Wash fish very well under cold water and pat dry; add salt and pepper.

STEP 2. Coat both sides of fish with flour. Turn the heat to high.

STEP 3. Place fry pan on the heat and add oil. When the pan becomes hot turn heat to medium and add the fish and fry until crispy on both sides (make sure fish is fully cooked); remove fish from pan and set aside. Fish is cooked when it flakes easily.

STEP 4. In a bowl mix vinegar, water, onion, carrots, hot pepper, and allspice; pour vinegar mixture in the same frying pan used to fry fish (make sure pan is still hot) and cook on medium heat for 15 minutes.

STEP 5. Pour liquid over fish; leave to soak into fish and marinate for a few hours at room temperature or overnight in the refrigerator.

Serve with Hardough Bread (found in many major grocery stores throughout North America; however, you will definitely find them in Caribbean or East Indian stores), or bammy (found in most Caribbean or East Indian stores). You can make this more of a meal by serving with rice or salad. This is a delicious way to cook fish.

Note: As I mentioned before, you can buy small red snappers and fry whole, increase cooking time, and use more flour, enough to coat fish.

Serves 4 people as a side dish.

SALT FISH BALLS (CODFISH BALLS)

These are great for a buffet or as an appetizer. Even if you don't believe in magic, these will disappear faster than you can cook them. The best part is that they are so easy to make. This recipe is a combination of several different recipes from family members and friends, which I made my own. This is pictured on pg 36. **SUBSTITUTE SALT FISH** with crab meat, lobster meat, or any white fish you like. ♥

- 2½–3 cups cooked salt fish (shredded and bones removed, or you can buy boneless salt fish)
- 5 medium potatoes boiled (peel and wash)
- 1 small onion (finely chopped)
- 2 small stalks of scallions (finely chopped)
- 1 tablespoon of fresh thyme (finely chopped) or 2 teaspoon's of ground thyme
- 3 tablespoons of fresh mint and or cilantro (finely chopped)
- 3 cloves of garlic (minced)
- 2 teaspoons of allspice
- 1 large egg (beaten)
- 1¼ cups of white (All purpose) flour
- 1½ teaspoons of baking powder
- salt and black pepper to taste
- vegetable oil for frying

COOKING AND PREPARATION INSTRUCTIONS

STEP 1. Peel, wash, and cut the potatoes in half. Turn the heat to medium. In a large pot with enough water to cover the potatoes; boil until fork tender. Drain potato and then mash with a fork or potato masher. Add the mashed potatoes to the shredded fish. Set aside and cool.

STEP 2. Add to the cooled potato mixture the onion, scallions, thyme, mint, garlic, allspice, and egg, and combine well.

STEP 3. In another bowl combine flour and baking powder. Add to the potato mixture slowly until it can easily be handled. **Taste for salt, and if needed, add salt at this stage and mix batter very well.** (It will always feel sticky, so have extra flour for dusting.)

STEP 4. Use two spoons to help form the mixture into balls. Turn the heat to medium.

STEP 5. Place fry pan on heat and fill halfway with oil. Add the balls to the hot oil and fry on each side until golden brown. Serve with your favorite dipping sauce. Makes about 15 balls.

Tip: When shallow frying or deep frying-To test if the oil is hot enough use a wooden spoon and place the bottom of the handle into the oil and if it bubbles around it— it's ready. The oil should reach about 350 to 375 degree F when deep frying— use a candy thermometer.

Note: Salt fish is very salty, so to remove the excess salt, you can either boil several times, changing the water after each boil, or you can soak overnight and then boil the salt fish for 15 minutes or until cooked. These can be prepared early in the day, and as your guests arrive, you can pop them into the oven; hot and crispy, with no stress. Freezes well; just remove from freezer and pop into the oven.

CURRY FISHCAKES

It doesn't get any better than this. These treats are full of flavor; the curry adds a flavor boost. I make my own, and I have met people who swear they don't like curry, but since trying mine, they are hooked. You have to find one that you like, and it may take time, but when you find it, you'll enjoy the pleasures of cooking with curry. This is also a recipe that Nanny the Great made one day on my first visit to Spanish Town. **SUBSITUTE WHITE FISH** with crab, lobster, or shrimp. ♥

- 2½–3 cups of fish (Boston blue, Pollock, or any white fish) (cooked and flaked)
- 5 medium potatoes (peel, wash, and boil until fork tender; mash and allow to cool)
- 1 small onion (finely chopped)
- 2 stalks of scallions (finely chopped)
- 5 cloves of garlic (finely chopped)
- 1 tablespoon of ginger (finely chopped)
- 2 tablespoons of curry (preferably a Caribbean, **Grace Products** or your choice)
- 1 tablespoon of fresh thyme (finely chopped)
- 1 large egg (beaten)
- 2 teaspoons of soya sauce (dark soya, mushroom flavored)
- 1½ cups of white (All purpose) flour
- 1½ teaspoons of baking powder
- salt and black pepper to taste
- 2 tablespoons of oil (your choice) + **vegetable oil for frying fishcakes**

COOKING AND PREPARATION INSTRUCTIONS

STEP 1. Peel, wash, and cut the potatoes in half. Turn the heat to medium. In a large pot with enough water to cover the potatoes; boil until fork tender. Drain potato and then mash with a fork or potato masher. Set aside and cool. Boil the fish, shred, and cool.

STEP 2. In a hot pan with 2 tablespoons of oil, add onion, scallions, garlic, and ginger, until translucent (3–4 minutes).

STEP 3. Add curry and cook for 2 more minutes, and then add thyme; set aside to cool.

STEP 4. In a large bowl add cooled mashed potatoes, flaked fish, egg, soya sauce, and the cooled seasonings from steps 2 and 3; mix well.

STEP 5. In a bowl combine flour, baking powder, salt, and black pepper; mix well, and then add to fish mixture. Combine all of the ingredients well and form mixture into cakes. If necessary, add more flour on your hands to help form cakes if mixture is too sticky. Keep about 1/3 cup of flour near you. Turn the heat to medium.

STEP 6. Place fry pan on heat and fill halfway with oil. Add the curry cakes to the hot oil and fry on each side until golden brown. Drain on paper towel and then serve. Makes about 12.

Tip: When shallow frying or deep frying-To test if the oil is hot enough use a wooden spoon and place the bottom of the handle into the oil and if it bubbles around it— it's ready. The oil should reach about 350 to 375 degree F when deep frying— use a candy thermometer.

Serve with mango and papaya chutney pg 17, fresh citrus sauce pg 16 or your favorite sauce. Top with tomato and pepper relish pg 14.

CURRY FISHCAKES WITH MANGO AND PAPAYA CHUTNEY (PG 17).

HOW NICE IT IS TO HAVE YOUR OWN MANGO TREE GROWING IN YOUR YARD. THAT'S GRANDPA, WHO LIVES IN SPANISH TOWN.

SALT FISH FRITTERS (STAMP AND GO)

These tasty treats not only smell delicious, but also taste equally as good. Just picture yourself with a nice cold drink underneath the sun eating one of these babies. Yummy! ♥

- 2½ to 3 cups of cooked salt fish (bones removed and shredded)
- 1 medium onion (finely chopped)
- 4 cloves of garlic (finely chopped)
- 2 stalks of scallions (finely chopped)
- 2 tablespoons of fresh mint (finely chopped)
- 1 tablespoon of fresh cilantro (optional)
- 1 to 2 teaspoons of scotch bonnet or your favorite hot pepper (finely chopped) **(optional)**
- 1 cup of white (All purpose) flour- sifted
- 1 teaspoon of baking powder
- 2 teaspoon of allspice
- ½ teaspoon of paprika
- 2 tablespoons of fresh thyme (finely chopped) or 1 teaspoon of ground thyme
- salt and black pepper to taste
- 1 large egg beaten
- 1 cup of cold water
- vegetable oil for frying fritters

COOKING AND PREPARATION INSTRUCTIONS

STEP 1.   In a large bowl put the onion, garlic, scallions, mint, cilantro, and hot pepper to the cooked and shredded salt fish.

STEP 2.   In another bowl add flour, baking powder, allspice, paprika, thyme, black pepper, and combine well.

STEP 3.   Add the flour mixture to the salt fish mixture, and then add egg and cold water to make a batter. Taste for salt. **If needed, add salt at this stage and mix batter very well.** Turn the heat to medium.

STEP 4.   Place fry pan on heat and fill halfway with oil. To the hot oil spoon in a scoop (about 1 tablespoon) of the batter and fry on each side until golden brown. (Fritters look like little pancakes) Drain on paper towel and transfer to plate. Makes about 12 fritters

Tip: When shallow frying or deep frying-To test if the oil is hot enough use a wooden spoon and place the bottom of the handle into the oil and if it bubbles around it— it's ready. The oil should reach about 350 to 375 degree F when deep frying— use a candy thermometer.

Note: Salt fish is very salty, so to remove the excess salt, you can either boil several times, changing the water after each boil, or you can soak overnight and then boil the salt fish for 15 minutes or until cooked. Great sauces would be spicy mango sauce pg 93, spicy mayo sauce pg 127, fresh citrus sauce pg 16, or your favorite.
SUBSTITUTE SALT FISH with crab meat, lobster meat, or any other white fish.

SALT FISH FRITTERS AND CODFISH BALLS

COOL SUMMER NIGHT IN JAMAICA, ALWAYS GOOD FOR A DRINK,
OR MAYBE TWO.

COCONUT SHRIMP

This is great for a buffet or as an appetizer. I love deep fried breaded shrimp, but when you add coconut to the mixture, yum and double yum. If you butterfly the shrimp, it helps cook the shrimp more evenly; just remember to leave the tails on. ♥

- 2 pounds of large shrimp (peel and de-vein) **(butterfly optional)**
- salt to taste
- ½ teaspoon of allspice
- vegetable oil for frying

BATTER
- ¾ cup of white (All purpose) flour
- 1 teaspoon of baking powder
- 1 large egg beaten
- ½ cup of beer

COATING
- ¾ cup of breadcrumbs (Japanese breadcrumbs if possible)
- 1½ cups of dried unsweetened coconut flakes
- 1 teaspoon of paprika
- 1½ tablespoons of garlic powder
- 2 teaspoons of allspice
- salt and black pepper to taste
- 2 teaspoons of fresh thyme (finely chopped) or 1 teaspoon of dried thyme

For the spicy palate-Add 1 teaspoon of ground chili, as long as you can handle it, no problem …

COOKING AND PREPARATION INSTRUCTIONS

STEP 1. **For shrimp:** You can leave shrimp as is, or you can butterfly. Slit shrimp down the back about ¾ of the way and spread apart, leaving tail on. In a bowl with the shrimp, combine salt, black pepper, and allspice; mix well.

STEP 2. **For batter:** In a bowl mix ¾ cup flour and baking powder. To the flour mixture, add the beaten egg and then the beer; mix well.

STEP 3. **Coating:** In another bowl combine all the ingredients to make the coating and mix well.

STEP 4. Dip shrimp individually into the batter and then roll in the coating. Turn the heat to medium.

STEP 5. Place fry pan or wok on heat and fill halfway with oil. Add the shrimps to the hot oil and fry on each side until golden brown. Place cooked shrimp on a plate lined with a paper towel to help drain excess oil. While hot, add more salt if desired.

Tip: When shallow frying or deep frying-To test if the oil is hot enough use a wooden spoon and place the bottom of the handle into the oil and if it bubbles around it— it's ready. The oil should reach about 350 to 375 degree F when deep frying— use a candy thermometer.

Great sauces from my book would be roasted red pepper sauce pg 16 or fresh citrus sauce pg 16. Serve with your favorite condiment.

AUNTIE WAH, MY CUTIE PIE, ANDREW JORDAN, & GRANDMA
FLETCHER.

ME WITH MY BEAUTIFUL JAMAICAN FAMILY—ALWAYS FESTIVAL
TIME.

SOUPS

The soups of Jamaica are unlike any other soups of the world; at least not any I have tried. My idea of soup consisted of chicken, vegetable, and beef; all neatly mixed in a convenient throwaway package. In other words, soups served as a starter, probably because of the quick time it took to prepare. Jamaican soups are hardy and served as meals, which bring new meaning to the age-old question, "Fork or spoon?" Whichever utensil you choose, these soups will satisfy the hardiest of appetites.

The legacy of the modern Jamaican soup started out like most great traditions—from the hands of the hard working agricultural worker. Back in those days, soup was served for the purpose of satisfying the tummy with a nutritious and filling meal. The soups contained a variety of meat, fish, potatoes, and dumplings. This was the birth of a tradition that continues today.

Jamaican soups are traditionally served on Saturday for lunch, because they take time to prepare, but are well worth the wait. Jamaican soups are meals served on their own; however, all can easily be turned into a starter by removing the meat bones and potatoes. You can serve the broth with small chunks of stewing meat or just the broth, as most Jamaican restaurants tend to do on the Island.

I remember the first time I served Pepperpot Soup to my husband (boyfriend at the time). I served the soup with the anticipation of praises. After all, I thought the soup was very good. I brought the soup to the table, and with a big smile, I boastfully placed the dish in front of my husband. What happened next was quite surprising. He asked me where the dumplings, meat, and potatoes were (or "Where's the beef?" for us culturally impaired). My husband was expecting Jamaican Pepperpot Soup; not a cream based vegetable soup. I understood what he meant the following Saturday when I went over to his mom's house. She was preparing Red Pea Soup. That was when I had my first awakening. I never saw soup with chunks of meat, potatoes, and dumplings. It was so delicious, and from that time on, Jamaican soups became part of my life. Now the only time I make chicken soup is when we are not feeling well, and for my son Andrew, who loves it. They may not be the prettiest looking soups, but the taste makes up for it. So take it from me; try these delicious soups that are prepared in the true Jamaican style with a slightly untraditional twist. When it comes to adding the root vegetables, you can choose a variety, such as white or yellow yams, Jamaican sweet potato, green banana, plantain, cho cho, dasheen, regular potato, and North American sweet potato. **Note**, anytime I mention milk in my recipes you can use, whole milk, low fat, skim, 1% and 2 % however the fatter the milk the better the end result

RED PEA SOUP

This soup is hardy and hard to resist. I refer to it as Jamaica's version of the chunky soup, but so much better. There are as many versions of this as there are Jamaicans. From house to house, the soup is made slightly differently, but they all end up with the same great taste. "Jamin', jamin' in the name of the Lord." This soup tastes better the next day, so it's a good thing to have leftovers. This is pictured on front cover. ♥

- 2 cups of dry red beans, or 1 can of red kidney beans (19 oz—540 ml)
- 10–12 cups of water (start with 10 cups and if needed, add the 2 cups)
- 8–9 sprigs of fresh thyme
- 2 teaspoons of ground thyme
- 2 cups of chopped carrots
- 1 small onion (finely chopped) **(optional)**
- 4 stalks of scallions (chopped)
- 7 cloves of garlic (finely chopped)
- $1\frac{1}{2}$ cups coconut milk **(optional)** (**Grace Products** or your choice)
- $\frac{1}{2}$ pound of ham hock or salted pig tail (cut into small pieces) **(optional) Wash well**
- $3\frac{1}{2}$–4 pounds of stewing beef + **2 pounds of beef soup bones Wash Well**
- 1 scotch bonnet or any hot pepper (whole)
- 5 cups of Jamaican sweet potatoes, yellow and or white yams cut into 2 inch pieces
- dumplings **(see page 22) See below for instructions**
- salt and black pepper to taste

COOKING AND PREPARATION INSTRUCTIONS

STEP 1. In a large pot add the red beans, water, thyme, onion, scallions, garlic, and coconut milk; add pot to the heat cook for $1\frac{1}{2}$ hours on medium heat, covered. Check occasional and stir to ensure beans aren't sticking.

STEP 2. After $1\frac{1}{2}$ hours add ham hocks or pig tail, stewing meat, soup bones, carrots and scotch bonnet pepper; cook covered for $1\frac{1}{2}$ hours more or until meat is tender. Add ground thyme and mix.

STEP 3. Before adding dumplings and root vegetables, make sure that the meat is cooked and tender. Add dumplings and cook for 15 minutes on medium heat, uncovered.

STEP 4. Season with salt and pepper to taste and then add root vegetables, and cook uncovered, until vegetables are fork tender and dumplings float to the top. Remove thyme stems and bones from soup. Soup should not be watery; see cover for consistency.

Dumplings for soups or stews are made long and thin referred to as spinners. With the palms of your hands facing each other, roll a piece of dough between them until you form a thin log about 3-4 inches long.

Note: If using canned beans, decrease cooking time to $\frac{1}{2}$ hour and cook uncovered in step 1. If using the salted pig tail, just like the salt fish, boil several times, changing water after each boil.

Although time consuming, you don't have to hover over the stove the entire time; check on it from time to time. I usually prepare on Saturday morning as I do my laundry. Yeah, I know, sounds exciting ... Yup, I know how to have fun!

ROXANNE, ENJOYING A BEAUTIFUL NIGHT OUT IN JAMAICA.

CALLALOO AND CRAB SOUP

This is another showstopper; a great way to start off a fancy dinner party. The sweetness of the crab really works well with the coconut milk, and with each taste, it helps me remember just how incredible the flavors of Jamaica are. This is pictured on pg 83. ♥

- 3 tablespoons of oil (your choice)
- 5–6 cloves of garlic (minced)
- 2 stalks of scallions (finely chopped)
- 1 small onion (finely chopped)
- 6–8 sprigs of thyme
- 15–20 pieces of okra (halved)
- 8 cups of callaloo or spinach (washed and shredded)
- 3 cups of coconut milk (**Grace Products** or your choice)
- 1 cup of milk (2% or 3%)
- $\frac{1}{2}$ scotch bonnet (finely chopped) **(optional)**
- 3–4 cups of cooked crab
- salt and black pepper to taste
- water

COOKING AND PERPARATION INSTRUCTIONS

STEP 1. In a large pot on medium heat, with 3 tablespoons of oil, fry garlic, scallions, and onion until soft; add thyme, and cook for a few minutes.

STEP 2. Add okra and callaloo or spinach, enough water or chicken stock to cover, and simmer gently for 5 minutes.

STEP 3. Add the milk and coconut milk and continue to cook on medium heat for a few more minutes.

STEP 4. Add the crabmeat and scotch bonnet; cover and cook on medium heat for 10 minutes.

STEP 5. Add salt and pepper; cook uncovered for 5 more minutes; remove soup from heat and pull thyme stems from soup with a fork. For a less chunky soup, you can blend, then add $\frac{1}{2}$ cup cream and reheat gently.

To add more flavor you can add 1-2 teaspoons of ground thyme in step 5.

Serves 4–6 people.

PEPPERPOT SOUP

Oh so good! This was the first Jamaican soup I ever had. It was at one of the beautiful Sandals resorts, and I was only served the broth and it was so amazing. Jamaican food is more than just satisfying your tummy; it's a way of life; it's a culture unlike any other. "Just give me the light." This is pictured on page 82.

- ➤ 10 cups of shredded callaloo or spinach
- ➤ 10 pieces of okra (halved)
- ➤ 10–12 cups of water (start with 10 cups and if needed add the 2 cups)
- ➤ ½ pound ham hocks (cut into small pieces) **(optional)**
- ➤ 3½ pounds of stewing beef + 1 pound of beef soup bones
- ➤ 4 stalks of scallions (finely chopped)
- ➤ 6 cloves of garlic (finely chopped)
- ➤ 7–8 sprigs of fresh thyme
- ➤ 1½–2 cups of coconut milk (**Grace Products** or your choice)
- ➤ 1 scotch bonnet **(optional)**
- ➤ 2 teaspoons of ground thyme
- ➤ salt and black pepper to taste
- ➤ Dumplings (See page 22) optional **See below for instructions**
- ➤ 6 cups of yellow, white yams, Jamaican sweet potatoes or green banana, chopped into 2–3-inch pieces (your choice; you can combine all of them or one or two that you like)

COOKING AND PREPARATION INSTRUCTIONS

STEP 1. Wash the callaloo or spinach, chop finely, and then set aside. Wash meat and bones thoroughly under cold running water.

STEP 2. In a pot add the water, ham hocks, stewing beef, beef bones, scallions, garlic, and thyme; cook on medium heat, covered, for about 1½ hours or until meat is tender.

STEP 3. Add coconut milk, scotch bonnet pepper, ground thyme, salt, and black pepper, and cook for another 30 minutes on medium heat, uncovered. If making dumplings add at this stage and cook for 15 minutes

STEP 4. Add okra, callaloo and your choice of root vegetable; cook for 10-15 minutes or until root vegetables are fork tender. Remove from heat and remove thyme stems from soup with a fork. If too thick, add more water and cook for a few minutes. Discard bones.

Soup should not be watery; same consistency as the red pea pictured on the cover and pumpkin soups.

Dumplings (See page 22) for soups are made long and thin referred to as spinners. With the palms of your hands facing each other, roll a piece of dough between them until you form a thin log about 3-4 inches long.

Serve in large bowl and "Everyting Irie."

Serves 4–6 people.

PUMPKIN SOUP (BEEF SOUP)

The pumpkin really gives this soup an extra delicious flavor. It really works. Trust me, make this one time and you will be hooked. I love the versatility with Jamaican soups. Sky's the limit! This is pictured on page 82. ♥

- 2½ pounds of soup bones
- 3½ pounds of beef stewing meat
- 10–12 cups of water (start with 10 cups and if needed add the 2 cups)
- 8 to 9 sprigs of thyme
- 6 cloves of garlic (finely chopped)
- 3 stalks of scallions (finely chopped)
- 1 scotch bonnet or your favorite hot pepper **(optional)**
- 2–2½ pounds of Caribbean (Jamaican) pumpkin (chopped into cubes)
- 1 chayote squash, also known as Cho Cho (sliced) **(optional)**
- boiled dumplings **(see page 22)**
- 1–2 packs of Jamaican pumpkin soup mix (most grocery stores in North American carry it, or you can buy it from a West Indian or Caribbean grocery store) **(optional)**
- 3 cups of Jamaican sweet potatoes (cubed, 2 inches)
- 2 cups of yellow yams (cubed, 2 inches)
- salt and black pepper to taste

COOKING AND PREPARATION INSTRUCTIONS

STEP 1. Under cold water wash soup bones and stewing beef really well. In a large pot add the water, soup bones, stewing meat, thyme, garlic, scallions, and hot pepper. Cook on medium heat with a tight fitting lid until meat is tender, about 1–1½ hours.

STEP 2. Add pumpkin and chayote squash; cook for 25–30 minutes more, covered.

STEP 3. Cut up Jamaican sweet potatoes and yellow yams; set aside in a bowl with cold water. This would also be a good time to make your dumplings

STEP 4. After about 25–30 minutes, pumpkin should be soft; mash the pumpkin with a wooden spoon and add dumplings, cook for 20 minutes more uncovered on medium heat. Add pumpkin soup mix and cook for 2 minutes.

STEP 5. Add sweet potatoes and yellow yams; cook uncovered for 10–15 more minutes, or until potatoes and yams are done. Add black pepper; check for salt, and if needed, add to soup. Soup should be thick in consistency, the same as the red pea and pepperpot soups.

Dumplings for soups are made long and thin referred to as spinners. With the palms of your hands facing each other, roll a piece of dough between them until you form a thin log about 3-4 inches long.

SUBSTITUTE JAMAICAN PUMPKIN with butternut squash or half Jamaican pumpkin and half butternut squash.

Serves 4–6 people.

PUREED PUMPKIN SOUP

This is another great way to start off a dinner party. Quick and easy and you will impress your guests. ♥

- 2 tablespoon's of oil (your choice olive, vegetable)
- 3 small stalks of scallions (finely chopped)
- 2 teaspoon's of fresh finely chopped ginger
- 2 teaspoons of ground thyme
- 4 cloves of garlic (minced)
- 5 cups of Caribbean (Jamaican) pumpkin (cut into 1-inch cubes)
- 1½ cups of butternut squash (cut into 1-inch cubes)
- ½–1 scotch bonnet pepper or your favorite hot pepper (finely chopped)
- 6 cups of chicken stock (canned stock will work) (you can use 3 cups water and 3 cups chicken stock)
- salt and black pepper to taste

COOKING AND PREPARATION INSTRUCTIONS

STEP 1. Turn the heat to medium. Place fry pan on heat and add the oil. Add the scallions, garlic, and ginger to the hot oil and sauté until soft. Add Jamaican pumpkin, butternut squash, and brown.

STEP 2. Add chicken stock, hot pepper, and thyme; cook on medium heat and bring to a boil.

STEP 3. Continue to cook covered until the pumpkin and butternut squash are soft and tender; this should take about 20 minutes.

STEP 4. Remove soup from heat and puree soup, season with salt and black pepper and return to pot and heat. You can add 1/3 cup cream for a creamier soup. Cook for 2 more minutes and remove from heat **(optional).**

Serve in a nice white bowl with a big smile!

Serves 4–6 people as a soup course.

RICE AND SALADS

Rice is very important to Jamaican cuisine; it's served with just about every savory dish. The most popular of the Jamaican rice dishes would be Rice and Peas; however, all of them are delicious. The noticeable difference with Jamaican rice dishes, other than the spices, is the time. These tasty dishes are not your traditional 5-minute recipes. As the women in Jamaica say, "Mi nuh wah nuh one-minute man." (Translation: I don't want no one-minute man.)

The importance of salads in Jamaican cuisine is not of high priority; however, the few they do have are so good, like the coleslaw and potato salad, which are commonly found in many Jamaican homes and restaurants. I have included one of my favorites: the seafood salad, jazzed up with Jamaican love. So enjoy any or all; you will definitely be glad you did. It's funny, what I have commonly seen served with most meals is your typical house salad served with either Thousand Island or French dressing—it seems to be a favorite with the Jamaicans that I know. So if you are running out of time, this would be a good option; the dressing really works well with Jamaican food.

PEACEFUL, AND OH SO BEAUTIFUL, THIS IS ONE OF THE REASONS WHY I LOVE JAMAICA, OTHER THAN THE FOOD, OF COURSE.

RICE AND PEAS

Lots of garlic along with scotch bonnet and coconut milk gives this rice dish a real jamin taste. I think that it's the tastiest of all the Caribbean rice dishes. See what you think! The quick version will not have the exact same color that rice and peas are known for but it will still have all the great taste. This is pictured on front the cover with roast beef. ♥

- 1 cup of canned red kidney beans
- 3 cups of water
- 1 cup of coconut milk (**Grace Products** or your choice)
- 4–5 cloves garlic (finely chopped)
- 6 sprigs of thyme
- 1 teaspoon of allspice and ground thyme (optional)
- 2 stalks of scallions (roughly chopped)
- 1 scotch bonnet pepper or your favorite hot pepper (whole or finely chopped) **(optional)**
- salt and black pepper to taste
- 2 cups of par-boiled white rice

COOKING AND PREPARATION INSTRUCTIONS

STEP 1. Drain liquid from can of beans into a bowl and set aside. Measure 1 can of coconut milk, water to make 3¾ cup then add liquid from can bean to measure 4 cups.

STEP 2. In a medium pot (2.5L/2½-qt.) put the 4 cups of liquid from step 1 then add garlic, thyme, scallions, and hot pepper, and cook on medium heat, uncovered, until it comes to a boil. Add salt and black pepper to taste; adjust seasonings.

STEP 3. Add rice, allspice, ground thyme give a mix and cook on simmer (low heat) covered for 20–30 minutes, until liquid has been absorbed. If necessary, mix occasionally toward the end to avoid sticking.

STEP 4. Turn heat off and cover for 5 minutes and fluff with fork to avoid lumps. Remove the thyme stems and any large pieces of scallions.

Tip: For more flavor fry the garlic and scallions in ¼ cup oil and then proceed with Step 2.

Traditionally, this is served with oxtail, curry dishes, and **many more.**

RICE AND PEAS (DRIED RED BEANS)

Always remember that when making rice, it's always 2 parts water to 1 part rice.

- 1 cup of dried kidney beans (washed well and soaked overnight)
- 5 cups of water + **1–2 cups, if needed**
- 6 cloves of garlic (finely chopped) + 1 clove of minced garlic
- 8 sprigs of thyme
- 3 stalks of scallions (roughly chopped) + 1 scallion finely chopped
- 1 scotch bonnet pepper or your favorite hot pepper (whole or finely chopped) **(optional)**
- 1¼ cups of coconut milk (**Grace Products** or your choice)
- 2 cups of par-boiled white rice
- 1 teaspoon each of ground thyme and allspice (optional)

- salt and black pepper to taste
- 3 tablespoons of oil (your choice)

COOKING AND PREPARATION INSTRUCTIONS

STEP 1. In medium pot (2.5L/2½-qt.) put the beans, water, garlic, thyme, scallions, and hot pepper, and cook on low heat, covered, for about 1½ hours, stirring occasionally.

STEP 2. When beans are tender (cooked) pour beans into a strainer and drain liquid into a bowl and reserve.

STEP 3. Measure the coconut milk and then add bean liquid to equal 4 cups, if necessary add more water.

STEP 4. Return pot to the stove turn heat to medium and add oil. When oil is hot add the minced garlic and finely chopped scallions and sauté for a few minutes. Add rice and mix for a few minutes and then add the ground thyme and allspice if using.

STEP 5. Add beans to the rice then add the bean liquid from step 3 and cook on simmer (low heat) covered for 20–30 minutes, until liquid has been absorbed. If necessary, mix occasionally toward the end to avoid sticking.

STEP 6. Turn heat off and cover for 5–10 minutes; fluff with fork to avoid lumps. Remove thyme stems with a fork.

Serves 4–6 people.

PORK FRIED RICE (JAMAICAN STYLE)

Jamaica has a large population of Asians; in fact, my husband's grandfather migrated to Jamaica from Hong Kong: "Out of many, one people". This is a favorite of kids, especially my son, who just loves it. This is another quick and easy meal for all those on the run. This is a great way to use your leftovers. ♥

- 2 tablespoons of oil (your choice)
- 2 stalks of scallions (finely chopped)
- 1 medium onion (finely chopped)
- 1 scotch bonnet pepper (finely chopped) **(optional)**
- 1 tablespoon of ginger (finely chopped)
- 2 cloves of garlic (finely chopped)
- 1 teaspoon of allspice
- 1 cup of chopped leftover roast pork or cooked ham steaks (chopped into small cubes or pieces)
- 1 red pepper (diced into small cubes)
- ½ cup of mixed vegetables (corn, peas, etc.)
- 1 egg **(optional)**
- 6 cups of cooked rice
- 3 tablespoons of soya sauce
- salt and black pepper to taste

COOKING AND PREPARATION INSTRUCTIONS

STEP 1.   In large fry pan or wok with 2 tablespoons of oil, on medium heat sauté the scallions, onion, hot pepper, ginger, and garlic; cook for 2 minutes.

STEP 2.   Add pork, red pepper, mixed vegetables, allspice and cook for 10 minutes, until pepper and vegetables are soft. Add egg to pan and stir until cooked and well incorporated.

STEP 3.   Add cooked rice; mix well, and then add soya sauce, salt, and black pepper, and mix until well combined and heated.

OPTION: Add 1 pound of shrimp to Step 1 for more of a meal.

This dish is commonly found on buffet tables in Jamaica. Serve with any fish or meat dish in this book.

Serves 4–6 people.

SEASONED RICE

This rice dish is a meal in itself, with salt fish and shrimp, it's all you need. This is a recipe from my late Nanny, with a twist or two. She was a wonderful lady and all who knew her loved her and thought she was an incredible cook. Spanish Town will never be the same without her. This is pictured on pg 84. ❤

- $3\frac{1}{2}$ cups of water
- 5 cloves of garlic (finely chopped)
- 1 tablespoon of fresh thyme (finely chopped)
- 3 stalks of scallions (finely chopped)
- 1 scotch bonnet pepper or your favorite hot pepper (whole or chopped) **(optional)**
- $\frac{1}{4}$ cup of coconut milk (**Grace Products** or your choice)
- $1\frac{1}{2}$ cups of cooked salt fish (shredded)
- 2 cups of rice
- salt and black pepper to taste
- 1 teaspoon of butter
- 1 pound of cooked shrimp (wash, peel, and de-vein, then cook)

COOKING AND PREPARATION INSTRUCTIONS

STEP 1. In a medium pot (2.5L/$2\frac{1}{2}$-qt.), add the water, garlic, thyme, scallions, hot pepper, and coconut milk, and bring this to a boil on medium heat.

STEP 2. Add salt fish and rice and continue to cook on medium to low heat, covered, for approximately 20–25 minutes or until water is absorbed.

STEP 3. Turn heat off and add cooked shrimp; cover for 5 minutes and then fluff with a fork. Taste for salt and black pepper.

SUBSTITUTE SALT FISH with any white fish or salmon.

Note: Salt fish is very salty, so to remove the excess salt, you can either boil several times, changing the water after each boil, or you can soak overnight and then boil the salt fish for 15 minutes or until cooked. Whichever method you choose, once the fish is cooked, shred (flake), so you have it ready to add to any dish.

Add a salad and you've got yourself a quick meal.

COCONUT INFUSED RICE WITH GARLIC AND THYME

- 3 cups of water
- 1 cup of coconut milk (**Grace Products** or your choice)
- 1 cup of shredded carrot
- 5 cloves of garlic (minced)
- 2 teaspoons of ground thyme
- 2 cups of par-boiled rice
- salt and black pepper to taste
- 3 tablespoons of oil your choice

COOKING AND PREPARATION INSTRUCTIONS

STEP 1. In a medium pot (2.5L/2½-qt.), add the oil and turn heat to medium. Add one 1 teaspoon of ground thyme and let cook in the oil for about 35 seconds. Add garlic and sauté for a few minutes then add the rice, the other teaspoon of thyme and carrots and mix well. Add the water, coconut milk, salt and black pepper to the rice.

STEP 2. Turn heat to low (simmer) and cook the rice covered, for approximately 20–25 minutes or until water is absorbed. Turn heat off and cover for 5 minutes and then fluff with a fork. Taste for salt and black pepper.

STIR FRIED NOODLES

This recipe was inspired by Rose, a friend of the family and one of the nicest people you will ever meet. ♥

- 1 package of Chow Mien noodles (350 g) (follow cooking directions on package)
- 2 stalks of scallions (finely chopped)
- 3 cloves of garlic (finely chopped)
- 1 tablespoon of fresh ginger (finely chopped)
- 1 green and red pepper (chopped into cubes)
- 1 cup of snow peas
- ½ cup of carrots (cut into thin slices)
- 1/3 cup of water or chicken broth
- 2 tablespoons each of sesame oil and oyster or hoisin sauce
- 1 tablespoon of dark soya sauce (preferably mushroom flavor)
- salt and black pepper
- 2 tablespoons of oil (your choice)

COOKING AND PREPARATION INSTRUCTIONS

STEP 1. In a large fry pan on medium heat, add the oil and sauté the scallions, garlic, and ginger for a few minutes.

STEP 2. Add red pepper, green pepper, snow peas, and carrots, and cook for 7–10 minutes, just until tender. Add sesame oil, soya sauce, oyster or hoisin sauce and black pepper to the vegetables and then add the noodles; mix well.

STEP 3. Add the water or chicken broth and cook until liquid is absorbed. Taste for salt, and if required, add more now; mix well and remove from heat. Serves 4 -6 people.

COLESLAW

I am not sure how this salad got introduced to Jamaica; however, it seems to be a side dish in many Jamaican restaurants and at family functions. ♥

- 4 cups of cabbage (shredded)
- 2 tablespoons white vinegar
- 2 tablespoons of oil (your choice)
- 1 cup of carrots (shredded)
- 1–1½ cups of light mayonnaise
- salt and black pepper to taste

COOKING AND PREPARATION INSTRUCTIONS

STEP 1.   Shred cabbage with a mandoline or slice very thin with a sharp knife.

STEP 2.   Combine shredded cabbage, vinegar, carrots, mayonnaise, salt, and black pepper, and mix well. Start with 1 cup mayonnaise, and then if not creamy enough, add the additional ½ cup and refrigerate for 2 hours or overnight.

This is really refreshing and is served with many dishes; it especially compliments spicy dishes.

Note: You can also add to the mayonnaise 2 teaspoons of ginger and garlic, 2 teaspoons of sesame oil, and 1 teaspoon of hot pepper for more of a kick.

You can also do an oil based dressing: 1/3 cup of oil, 3 tablespoons of vinegar, 1 tablespoon of sesame oil, 2 teaspoons of garlic minced and 2 teaspoons of ginger. I also like to add fresh chopped cilantro. Mix well and pour on cabbage.

Serves 4–6 people.

POTATO SALAD

This is my mother-in-law's recipe and one of the best potato salads ever. This is simplicity at its best. This is pictured on pg 82. ♥

- ➤ 8 large potatoes (boiled)
- ➤ 2 tablespoons of butter or oil
- ➤ 2 tablespoons of white vinegar
- ➤ 2 scallions (finely chopped)
- ➤ 1 celery stalk (finely chopped)
- ➤ 1 cup of cooked peas (frozen or canned)
- ➤ 4 large boiled eggs (chopped)
- ➤ 1–1½ cups of light or regular mayonnaise (for more of a creamier salad, add 2 cups)
- ➤ salt and black pepper to taste

COOKING AND PREPARATION INSTRUCTIONS

STEP 1.   In a large pot put the cubed potatoes, enough water to cover, and add salt.

STEP 2.   Cook on medium heat for 20 minutes or until potatoes are tender.

STEP 3.   In a large bowl put the cooked potatoes, butter or oil, vinegar, celery and scallion; mix well. Add peas and eggs and mix well, and cool for approximately 10 minutes.

STEP 4.   While still hot, add mayonnaise, and a pinch of pepper and salt to taste. Let cool and then refrigerate.

This salad is good with just about any meat or fish dish.

This is a very popular dish at parties. I have many requests for this salad.

Serves 4–6 people.

GRILLED SEAFOOD SALAD

This is such a delicious and refreshing salad and really great as a light lunch. This is one of my favorite salads and one that I enjoy all the time. Again, I took a classic recipe and added lots of flavor, Jamaican style. Man, I tell you, it doesn't get any better. This is pictured on pg 82. ♥

- 1½ pounds of squid (bodies and tentacles cleaned)
- 1½ pounds of medium shrimp (washed, de-veined, and peeled)
- 1 pound of sea scallops
- 4 cloves of garlic (minced)
- 2 teaspoons of fresh ginger (finely chopped)
- ½ teaspoon of allspice
- 1 teaspoon of fresh thyme (finely chopped)
- 2 tablespoons of fresh mint (finely chopped)
- ½ cup oil (your choice)
- ¼–1/3 cup of white vinegar
- 2–3 tablespoons of fresh lime juice
- salt and black pepper
- 1 onion (thinly sliced)
- 1 green pepper (thinly sliced)
- lettuce and cucumber

COOKING AND PREPARATION INSTRUCTIONS

STEP 1.   Combine together garlic, ginger, allspice, thyme, mint, oil, vinegar, lime juice, salt, and black pepper; whisk and set aside.

STEP 2.   Preheat barbeque to medium and make sure to grease the grill to avoid sticking.

STEP 3.   Grill squid, shrimp, and scallops for about 2 minutes per side or until cooked.

STEP 4.   Cut squid into rings and cut scallops and shrimp in half.

STEP 5.   In a bowl, put the squid, shrimp, scallops, green pepper, and onions, and pour the dressing over the fish. (Refrigerate for 1–2 hours, or for best results, overnight.)

On a platter, arrange your favorite lettuce and cucumber and pour seafood salad; sprinkle more mint on top. If you like it hot, add some scotch bonnet pepper to the vinegar mixture in Step 1.

OPTIONAL: If you can't get to a grill you can boil the seafood.

If watching your fat intake, reduce oil to 1/3 and add more lime juice and ginger for more flavor.

Serves 4–6 people.

CRAB SALAD IN PAPAYA

I had this for the first time at Sandals Dunns River and I loved it so much. I hope my version becomes one of your favorites too. It is great as an appetizer and it's quick and easy. This is pictured on pg 83. ❤

> ➢ 3 cups of cooked crab (shredded; use king crab legs or meat from whole crab)
> ➢ 2 stalks of scallions (finely chopped)
> ➢ 2 cloves of garlic (minced)
> ➢ 1 tablespoon of fresh thyme (finely chopped)
> ➢ 2 tablespoons of fresh mint or cilantro or both (finely chopped)
> ➢ 1/3 cup of oil (your choice)
> ➢ salt and black pepper to taste
> ➢ 2 tablespoons of fresh lime juice
> ➢ 2 tablespoons of white vinegar
> ➢ 2 medium papayas (cut into halves and seeds removed)

COOKING AND PREPARATION INSTRUCTIONS

STEP 1.   In a bowl with the crab, add scallions, garlic, thyme, mint, oil, salt, pepper, lime juice, and vinegar; mix well. Cover and marinate for 1 hour or overnight in the fridge.

STEP 2.   Meanwhile, cut papaya in half and remove seeds. Remove crab mixture from fridge.

STEP 3.   Fill each half of the papaya with crab mixture and sprinkle with more mint or cilantro on top. Serve and enjoy!

Note: You can also add basil or parsley to the mix; not typically Jamaican, but it does add good flavor.

Serves 4 people.

Vito by the pool enjoying the wonderful weather down in Ochi.

GRILLED VEGETABLE AND CHICKEN SALAD SERVED WITH GRILLED BREAD

As I said, you can never forget your roots. I took the classic Italian grilled vegetable and chicken salad and added the flavor of Jamaica. I love to grill and it is a much healthier way to enjoy any type of food, especially given the health conscious world we will live in. This is really easy, so don't let the long list of ingredients, or the preparation instructions scare you off. ♥

- ➢ 4 chicken breasts
- ➢ 1 teaspoon of fresh thyme (finely chopped) or ½ teaspoon of dried thyme
- ➢ 3 cloves of garlic (minced)
- ➢ 1 teaspoon of ginger (finely chopped)
- ➢ ¼ cup of oil (your choice)
- ➢ salt and pepper
- ➢ 6 large white mushrooms
- ➢ 4 large red peppers or yellow pepper, or both, halved (remove seeds and stems)
- ➢ 4 large carrots, sliced in halves
- ➢ 1/3 cup of olive oil (or your choice) + ¼ **cup oil** for brushing on vegetables before grilling
- ➢ 2 cloves of garlic (minced)
- ➢ 1 teaspoon of fresh ginger (finely chopped)
- ➢ 1 teaspoon of fresh mint (finely chopped)
- ➢ 1 tablespoon of fresh lime juice + 1 lime
- ➢ salt and black pepper
- ➢ 1 loaf of bread (French stick)

COOKING AND PREPARATION INSTRUCTIONS

STEP 1. In a small bowl combine chicken with 1 teaspoon of thyme, 3 cloves of garlic, 1 teaspoon of ginger, ¼ cup of oil, salt, and pepper. Refrigerate 2–3 hours or overnight.

STEP 2. Wash vegetables well. In a large bowl put the vegetable and drizzle with ¼ cup of oil, ensuring that all the vegetable are well coated. Preheat barbeque to medium and make sure to grease the grill to avoid sticking.

STEP 3. Grill peppers until charred on all sides; remove from grill and place in a bowl and cover with plastic wrap. Allow to cool and then remove skins. Set aside. Combine together 1/3 cup oil, garlic, ginger, mint, lime juice, black pepper, and salt; whisk and set aside.

STEP 4. Grill on medium heat the carrots for about 5–10 minutes and then add mushrooms and grill for 5 minutes or until soft. Remove from the grill. Slice peppers, carrots, and mushrooms; place in a large bowl and add the marinade from **Step 4** and refrigerate 2–3 hours or overnight.

STEP 5. Remove chicken from fridge and turn the grill on medium heat then grease with oil to avoid sticking. Grill with the lid closed for 5-7 minutes per side or until fully cooked. Remove from heat and set aside to cool. Slice chicken into diagonal slices.

STEP 6. Cut bread into diagonal slices; brush oil on both sides of the bread and grill for 2 minutes on medium heat.

STEP 7. On a large platter place vegetables and top with the chicken slices; drizzle more oil and lime juice and then arrange the bread.

VEGETABLES AND SANDWICHES

Many, if not all, of the recipes in this section are Jamaican inspired, using ingredients commonly used in Jamaican cuisine. These are my interpretations of delicious food I have had on my visits to the Island. I love the way Jamaicans season their food, so I took the common vegetable, and sandwich, and gave it more love with the exotic spice of Jamaica. So I hope many of these recipes will grace your table so your family and friends can enjoy them for many years to come. The importance of vegetables in Jamaican cuisine is not of high priority; however, the few they do have are so good, like callaloo, ackee, and plantain. You can impress your guests with the Island Love Mashed Sweet Potato or the Grilled Corn, to mention a few. Remember, it is old Jamaica meets new Jamaica meets me. I will be tempting you to try everything.

I CAN REMEMBER TAKING THIS PICTURE THINKING HOW BEAUTIFUL AND PERFECT IT IS HERE AND IT ONLY MADE IT MUCH HARDER FOR ME TO HAVE TO LEAVE.

STEAMED CALLALOO

This is my version of callaloo, which is served throughout Jamaica. This is quick and easy.

- 11 cups of callaloo or spinach (wash well, dry, and shred)
- ¼ cup of oil (your choice)
- 3 cloves of garlic (minced)
- 2 stalks of scallions (finely chopped)
- 1 small onion (finely chopped)
- 1 teaspoon of fresh thyme (finely chopped)
- 2 cups of roughly chopped tomato's
- 1/3 cup of coconut milk (**Grace Products** or your choice) or you can use water
- 2 tablespoons of fresh lime juice
- salt and black pepper to taste

COOKING AND PREPARATION INSTRUCTIONS

STEP 1.　In a pot on medium heat, add the oil and sauté the garlic, scallions, onion, and thyme for 3 minutes. Add coconut milk or water, tomato's and then the callaloo or spinach; and continue to cook covered on medium heat until wilted. Add salt, pepper, and lime juice; cook for 10 to 12 more minutes.

STEP 2.　Continue to cook uncovered for 2 more minutes. Remove from heat and transfer onto a serving dish. Season with salt and pepper.

Serve with grilled steak pg 74, roast beef 88, grilled boneless roast pork pg 92, pick up salt fish pg 116 or any grilled fish dish.

SUBSTITUTE- SPINACH

ACKEE WITH BOILED DUMPLINGS AND GREEN BANANAS

This is a really good and quick meal. As I mentioned earlier, the dumplings and bananas are integral partners in this dish. You cannot have one without the other. ♥

- 2 cans of ackee (sold in most grocery stores or in West Indian stores, canned) (**Grace Products**)
- 1/3 cup of oil (vegetable); olive oil will change the taste
- 3 stalks of scallions (finely chopped)
- 1 onion (cut into thin slices)
- 1 green pepper (thinly sliced)
- 2 cups of tomatoes (roughly chopped)
- 1 whole scotch bonnet pepper
- salt and black pepper
- boiled dumplings (see pg22)
- 4–6 green bananas

COOKING AND PREPARATION INSTRUCTIONS

STEP 1. Prepare dumplings (see page 22) and peel green bananas and add to a large pot with enough water to cover the dumplings and bananas. Cook on medium heat for about 15 minutes or until dumplings float to the surface and bananas are fork tender. Keep warm.

STEP 2. Meantime, place fry pan on medium heat and add oil. Add the scallions, onion, and green pepper to hot oil and cook until tender.

STEP 3. Add tomatoes and scotch bonnet and cook for 1 more minute. Add ackee; cook for 10 more minutes until heated through. Add salt and pepper, and taste for seasonings.

On individual plates, scoop the ackee mixture over dumplings and green bananas. Serve about 2 dumplings and 1 or 2 green bananas per person. Also great with this dish is the steamed callaloo.

TIP- Peel green banana's, and add to a pot of boiling salted water and cook for 15-20 minutes, or until tender. Green bananas can be difficult to peel, so to make things easier, wash the bananas really well, and with a sharp knife cut the ends. Then run the knife in the middle of the green banana and make a slit in the peel— do not cut into the green banana just the peel! In a pot with boiling salted water add 2 tablespoons of milk and then add your green bananas; cook for 20 minutes or until fork tender. Adding the milk will help avoid staining in your pot. Thanks for the great tip Phillis!

OPTIONAL: You can serve with fried dumplings or over rice.

Serves 4-6 people.

ISLAND LOVE MASHED SWEET POTATOES

This is really good and a classy addition to any formal dinner. The flavors really work well together, and let's face it; you can't go wrong with sweet potatoes. This is pictured on pg 82 with the grilled steak. ♥

- 6 medium sweet potatoes or regular potatoes (Yukon gold)
- 4 tablespoons of oil (your choice)
- 1 onion (thinly sliced)
- 2 cloves of minced garlic
- 1 tablespoon of fresh thyme (finely chopped)
- 2 tablespoons of butter
- ½–1 cup of cream or (2% milk)
- salt and black pepper to taste

COOKING AND PREPARATION INSTRUCTIONS

STEP 1.   Boil or bake sweet potatoes until tender; mash and set aside.
STEP 2.   Meantime, place fry pan on medium heat and add oil. Add onion to hot oil and cook until golden brown, about 10 to 12 minutes. Add garlic, thyme and cook for a few minutes more.
STEP 3.   In a large pot put the potatoes, onion mixture, butter, salt and black pepper and cream, and cook over low heat for 5 minutes, stirring constantly until creamy.

Serve with any grilled or baked meat dish, and many more.

SWEET POTATO WEDGES

My mom cooks this for us with Yukon potatoes with Italians spices. I took her recipe and added Island spices. Delicious! This is pictured on pg 83 with special hut burger.

- 5 medium sweet potatoes or Yukon gold potatoes
- 2 teaspoon's of ground tyme
- salt and black pepper to taste
- 1 teaspoon of allspice
- 1 tablespoon of garlic powder
- ¼ cup of oil (your choice)

COOKING AND PREPARATION INSTRUCTIONS

STEP 1.   Cut sweet potatoes into wedges about 2-inch thick.
STEP 2.   In a bowl combine wedges with thyme, salt, black pepper, allspice, garlic powder; mix well.
STEP 3.   Preheat oven to 400 degrees; on an oiled cookie sheet, spread sweet potatoes or regular potatoes in a single layer and drizzle generously with oil and cook for approximately 15-25 minutes, turning once, until golden and crispy.

This is great with special hut burger pg 77 or oven roasted ribs pg 85.

SPICED FRENCH FRIES

I just gave a little life to the ordinary French fried potato. I bet you will be glad that I did. ♥

- 6 large potatoes
- 1 teaspoon of allspice
- 1 teaspoon of ground thyme
- 2 teaspoons of paprika
- 1 teaspoon of cayenne pepper (optional-if you like it spicy)
- salt and black pepper to taste
- oil for frying

COOKING AND PREPARATION INSTRUCTIONS

STEP 1. Wash potatoes and peel. In a small bowl combine allspice, thyme, paprika, salt, and black pepper; mix gently and set aside.

STEP 2. Cut into strips using a knife or French fry cutter and soak strips in cold water for about 5–10 minutes. Drain and dry strips thoroughly.

STEP 3. There are two frying stages:
First heat vegetable oil to 325°F/160°C in a deep fryer or deep pot. Fry the potatoes in batches until lightly browned and limp about 5 minutes. Drain on paper towels. This is called blanching

STEP 4. **Second** increase the temperature of the oil to 375°F/190°C, put the potatoes, in batches, back into the oil and fry until brown and crisp. Remove the fries from the oil with a slotted spoon to a plate lined with paper towels and immediately season with the spice mixture.

OPTION: You can bake in a 350 degree oven on a baking sheet lined with parchment paper; grease generously with oil. Place potatoes on a single layer and bake until golden and crispy.

Tip: If you don't have a candy thermometer you can test if the oil is hot enough by using a wooden spoon and place the bottom of the handle into the oil and if it bubbles around it— it's ready

SUBSTITUTE POTATOES with sweet potatoes.

Great with special hut burger pg 77 or oven roasted ribs pg 85.

GRILLED CORN

This is so good! That's all I have to say; if you like corn, then give this a try. ♥

- 6 ears corn on the cob (halved)
- 1/3 cup of unsalted butter
- 1 teaspoon of ground thyme or 2 teaspoons of fresh thyme (finely chopped)
- ½ teaspoon of allspice
- 3 tablespoons of fresh lime juice
- salt and black pepper **(optional)**

COOKING AND PREPARATION INSTRUCTIONS

STEP 1.   Remove the husk from corn; Preheat grill to medium or high. Be sure to grease the grill to avoid sticking. Put the corn on the hot grill.

STEP 2.   Melt butter; add thyme, allspice, **salt, black pepper (optional)**, and lime juice, and mix well.

STEP 3.   Generously brush butter mixture onto corn and grill for approximately 10-15 minutes, turning often.

Serve with just about any meat dish or grilled fish and seafood in this book.

Serves 6 people.

PLANTAINS

Traditionally, plantains are prepared for breakfast and served hot, but you can enjoy them with any meal. I love preparing fried plantains, because their smell always brings me back to Spanish Town, Jamaica, even in the middle of winter. The smell is so intoxicating, like the smell of summer flowers in a mild summer breeze. This is pictured on pg 82 with the spicy chili garlic steak. ♥

- 3 plantains (should be ripe; when ripe, skin peels off easily)
- 1/3 to ½ cup of oil (vegetable or corn)
- salt to taste (optional)

COOKING AND PREPARATION INSTRUCTIONS

STEP 1.   Peel plantains and slice on a diagonal, about ½-inch thick.

STEP 2.   Turn the heat to medium. Place fry pan on heat and add the oil. Add the plantains gently in the hot oil; fry until golden on both sides.

STEP 3.   Place cooked plantains on a dish layered with paper towels to soak up excess oil.

While plantains are hot you can sprinkle with salt or nutmeg or with nothing at all   your choice. That's the great thing about cooking; you're the boss!

Serve with many Jamaican dishes or enjoy them on their own. Plantains really complement spicy dishes, as the sweetness of the plantain cuts the heat of the hot pepper.

OPTION: Plantains can also be grilled. Brush with oil on both sides and grill 3–4 minutes per side. This is a healthier way to prepare them. Plantains can also be cut into 3 portions and boiled for about 10–15 minutes or until fork tender.

Tip: To test if the oil is hot enough use a wooden spoon and place the bottom of the handle into the oil and if it bubbles around it— it's ready. The oil should reach about 350 to 375 degree F when deep frying— use a candy thermometer.

Note: If in doubt whether a plantain is ripe, you can ask your produce person; they will be glad to help. Try to find a plantain that has a yellowish color that is slightly bruised. The plantain is at it's sweetest when it is fully black. If this stage is not available in your grocery store, you can place the plantain in a paper bag until it turns black. You don't want to use a plantain when it is green, it will not be sweet in fact it will be starchy and its taste will be comparable to a potato.

JAM DOWN CRAB SANDWICH

I love this sandwich; crab with a touch of ginger really gives spice to life. You will be thanking me with each bite you take. No worries in Jamaica. Enjoy! This is quick and easy. ♥

* 3 cups of cooked, shredded crab (king crab legs or meat from whole crab)
* 1/3 cup of light mayonnaise (for creamier sandwich use ½ cup)
* 1 tablespoon of oil (your choice)
* ½ teaspoon of fresh thyme (finely chopped)
* 1–2 teaspoons of fresh ginger (finely chopped)
* 3 tablespoons of fresh lime juice + 1 teaspoon of lime zest
* 2 tablespoons of fresh mint (finely chopped)
* salt and black pepper
* 2 ripe avocados
* hardough or any type of bread, such as white toast bread, buns, or even on a flatbread

COOKING AND PREPARATION INSTRUCTIONS

STEP 1.   In a small bowl combine mayonnaise, oil, thyme, ginger, lime, lime zest, black pepper and mint.

STEP 2.   Add mayonnaise mixture to the crabmeat and mix well. Add salt if desired, and mix well.

STEP 3.   Halve avocado, remove pit, and then slice.

STEP 4.   Spread crabmeat on bread and arrange avocado on top.

If you are watching your weight you can reduce mayo to ¼ cup and add more lime.

Serve with coleslaw pg 53, potato salad pg 54, or with a fresh salad. Enjoy with a cold drink, such as a cooler or red stripe beer!

Note: You can use imitation crab; it's much more economical; however, I find it too sweet.

Serves 3–4 people.

JAM DOWN CRAB SANDWICH, SERVED WITH COLESLAW

SHOWN HERE WITH MY LITTLE PRINCE IS HIS AUNTIE JODY, ON
THEIR WAY FOR A QUICK AND DELICIOUS LUNCH.

GRILLED CHICKEN SANDWICH WITH LIME AND MINT MAYO

This is grilled chicken at its best; just when you thought you had it figured out, along comes Mary with this fabulous sandwich. This is great for a quick meal, so you can enjoy the beautiful summer's day. It's all about time. This is pictured on pg 84. ❤

- 4 chicken breasts fillets you can purchase in most grocery stores or butterfly a chicken breast until it opens open like a book and then just cut straight down for two separate pieces.
- 4 cloves of garlic (minced)
- 1 teaspoon of fresh ginger (finely chopped)
- 5 sprigs of fresh thyme (finely chopped)
- 2 tablespoons of fresh lime juice
- ¼ cup of oil (your choice)
- salt and black pepper to taste
- 1 scotch bonnet (finely chopped) **(optional)**
- 4 crusty buns
- shredded lettuce
- 2 tomatoes (sliced)
- 2 avocados (sliced)
- **LIME AND MINT MAYO**
- 6 tablespoons of mayonnaise
- 2 tablespoons of oil
- 1 tablespoon of chopped mint
- 3 tablespoons of lime juice
- 1 tablespoon of hot sauce (optional)

COOKING AND PREPARATION INSTRUCTIONS

STEP 1.   In a large bowl combine garlic, ginger, thyme, lime juice, oil, salt, black pepper, and scotch bonnet pepper, and mix well. Place chicken in mixture and thoroughly coat; cover and refrigerate for 2 hours or overnight.

STEP 2.   Grill chicken on a greased grill on medium heat; close lid. Cook chicken until no longer pink, around 3 to 4 minute per side. Allow to cool. When done, juices will run clear when a fork is inserted.

STEP 3.   **Lime and mint mayo-** Combine mayonnaise, oil, mint, and lime juice together; mix well.

STEP 4.   Cut buns in half and grill about 1 minute. Spread mayo on one side; add chicken, lettuce, tomato, and avocado.

SUBSTITUTE THE MAYO- with fresh garlic and thyme sauce on pg 17 or with an oiled based dressing.
- 5 tablespoons of oil (your choice)
- 1 teaspoon of vinegar and **chopped mint**
- 2 tablespoons of lime juice

COOKING AND PREPARATION INSTRUCTIONS

Combine all ingredients and mix very well; pour over bread or chicken.

SHOWN HERE IS MY SISTER WITH MY NIECES ELISABETH AND
SAMANTHA; ALL READY TO GET SOMETHING DELICIOUS TO EAT.

MORE BIG SMILES AFTER A WONDERFUL MEAL AT JADE GARDEN IN
JAMAICA.

BEEF, POULTRY, GOAT, AND LAMB

One thing I can tell you for sure about Jamaicans, they love their meat. As I mentioned earlier, vegetables are strictly served as a side dish. I often joke with my husband regarding the hardy, stick to your stomach meals that I have come to love, such as Stewed Peas, Oxtail Stew, and Curry Chicken, just to mention a few. All of the recipes will open up your senses and awaken you to the exotic tastes that are all easy to prepare. I have included most of the traditional recipes and many more, all Jamaican inspired. You can impress your friends with tasty delights such as Jerk Dishes, Curry Dishes, and Grilled Chicken with Pineapple Kebobs. For me, the best thing of all is that Jamaicans season (marinate) most of the dishes the night before, so all you have to do is cook it when you're ready the next day. Marinating the meat will also enhance the flavors, but don't get too excited if you don't remember or have the time; it will still taste great without marinating. I usually marinate the night before. I get all my ingredients, which usually are thyme, scallions, garlic, onion, scotch bonnet **(optional)**, and ginger, and put them all into my food processor. In less than 1 minute, all are chopped up. It's easy, so don't let the long list of ingredients scare you off, because as I mentioned earlier in this book, they are roughly chopped. The unique blend of flavors is what really makes the dishes taste great. You can see (as well as taste) the Indian, Asian, and European flavors with the ingredients that I mentioned above and the presence of soya sauce (dark), allspice, and curry. You can use a re-sealable bag to marinate any of the dishes, this makes for easier cleanup. **When barbequing always grease the grill to avoid sticking (you can use oil or a cooking spray which ever is easiest).** So please, come discover. Or for those of you who are Jamaican but lost touch with your native foods; let's rediscover the wonderful world of Jamaican food!

IT IS ALL REALLY KIND OF LIKE MAGIC—THE FOOD, THE PLACE, THE PEOPLE, THE SOUNDS; ALL OF IT—THE PASSION.

STEWED PEAS

This is Jamaica's version of beef stew with a whole lot of flavor. This does take some time, but anything good is always worth the wait. ♥

- ➤ 1 cup of dried red beans
- ➤ 8 sprigs of fresh thyme
- ➤ 2 teaspoons of ground thyme
- ➤ 1 medium onion (chopped)
- ➤ 3 stalks of scallions (finely chopped)
- ➤ 5 cloves of garlic (finely chopped)
- ➤ 4½ cups of water + (additional water if necessary)
- ➤ 1 pound of ham hocks, or pig tails cut into small pieces (substitute with 1 pound of pork bones)
- ➤ 3½ pounds of stewing meat (most grocery stores have it packaged)
- ➤ 1 scotch bonnet pepper or any hot pepper (finely chopped) **(optional)**
- ➤ salt and black pepper to taste
- ➤ boiled dumplings (page 22); shape them thin and small (reduce recipe to half)
- ➤ ½ cup of coconut milk **(Grace Products or your choice)** (or substitute with 2 tablespoons of butter)
- ➤ cornstarch (if necessary)

COOKING AND PREPARATION INSTRUCTIONS

STEP 1. Wash meat thoroughly under cold running water and refrigerate until ready to add to the stew. Add beans, thyme, ground thyme, onion, scallions, garlic, and water in a large pot. Cook on low heat (simmer) for 1½ hours covered. Stir occasionally.

STEP 2. Meantime, make dumplings (see page 22); set aside. For soups and stews dumplings are made long and thin referred to as spinners. With the palms of your hands facing each other, roll a piece of dough between them until you form a thin log about 3-4 inches long.

STEP 3. Add ham hocks, pig tails, stewing meat, scotch bonnet, salt, black pepper, dumplings, and coconut milk; simmer for an additional 1 hour, covered. Cook until meat is tender. Stir occasionally, and if necessary add more water.

STEP 4. Continue to cook, uncovered on medium heat for 30 more minutes or until the liquid in the pot thickens. Never allow the liquid to completely absorb, you should always check for enough liquid in the pot. Check for salt and adjust seasonings if necessary. Remove thyme stems and serve over rice.

Tip: If the liquid is still too watery, add 2-3 tablespoons of cornstarch and mix it with enough water until it has the consistency of heavy cream (smooth). While on medium heat, remove meat from pot. Add flour mixture to the pot slowly until it thickens. Mix well to avoid lumps, and then pour sauce over meat

Note: If using salted pig tails, just like the salt fish, boil several times, changing the water after each boil. This is a stew so make sure to have enough gravy.

Serves 4 people.

STEWED PEAS AND SPINNERS WITH PLAIN RICE

HERE ARE A FEW OF THE WOMEN WHO INSPIRED ME TO MAKE GREAT JAMAICAN DISHES: MY AUNTIE SANNIE, MOTHER-IN-LAW, MARCIA, PHILLIS, AND LORNA, ENJOYING A DAY UNDER THE BRIGHT JAMAICAN SUN.

GRILLED STEAK

This is so easy to prepare and it is so good. This is a hit with all men who love meat. "No woman, no cry"—the ladies will love this too. This is another great way to enjoy the outdoors with the added bonus of the intoxicating aroma this steak will release. Feel the breeze! This is another quick dish that is a hit with kids too. This is pictured on page 82. ♥

- 4 steaks (sirloin, rib eye, T-bone, or your choice; about 1" thick)
- 2–3 tablespoons of fresh thyme (finely chopped)
- 3 stalks of scallions (finely chopped)
- 1 tablespoon of fresh ginger (finely chopped)
- 2 teaspoons of allspice
- 2 tablespoons of soya sauce
- 1 scotch bonnet pepper or any hot pepper (finely chopped) **(optional)**
- 4 cloves of garlic (minced)
- 2 tablespoons of rum (**Appleton Jamaica Rum** or your choice) **(optional)**
- 1/3 cup of oil (your choice) you can use less ¼ cup
- salt and black pepper to taste
- 2 tablespoons of fresh lime juice

COOKING AND PREPARATION INSTRUCTIONS

STEP 1. In a bowl combine thyme, scallions, ginger, allspice, soya sauce, scotch bonnet, garlic, rum, oil, salt, and black pepper, and mix well. Pour sauce all over the steaks and marinate for 2 hours or overnight in fridge.

STEP 2. Remove steaks from fridge bring them down to room temperature (optional) and squeeze lime on them.

STEP 3. Fire up the grill on medium or high and grease the grill to avoid sticking. Grill the steak with the lid closed for 5 minutes then turn steak over and continue to cook for few more minutes or until your preference. Remember, anything over medium dries the meat. Place meat on a dish, cover with foil, and let sit for 5 minutes.

Serve with Island love mashed sweet potatoes pg 62 or with any rice dish from this book. Another great side dish would be seasonal vegetables.

Note: If you want more color on your steak pat dry the steaks before you place them on the grill.

Use any prepared sauce, or you can choose healthier and more delicious alternatives like the papaya mint salsa, mango salsa, avocado and tomato salsa, roasted red pepper sauce, mango and papaya chutney, or fresh garlic and thyme sauce, found on pg 14, 15, 16, and 17.

Feel the breeze! Add a red stripe beer and you have a nice, casual lunch. "Everyting irie!"

Serves 4 people.

SPICY CHILI GARLIC STEAK

My father-in-law, who is a great Jamaican cook, inspired this steak dish. I love steak prepared this way and I'm sure you will too. This is pictured on page 82. ♥

- ➤ 4 steaks (sirloin, rib eye, T-bone, or your choice; about 1" thick)
- ➤ 2 tablespoons of fresh thyme (finely chopped)
- ➤ 3 stalks of scallions (finely chopped)
- ➤ 1 small onion (cut into cubes)
- ➤ ½ teaspoon of allspice
- ➤ 2 tablespoons of soya sauce
- ➤ 1 tablespoon of fresh ginger (finely chopped)
- ➤ 8 tablespoons of hoisin sauce
- ➤ 4 tablespoons of chili-garlic sauce, sold in all major grocery stores
- ➤ 4 cloves of garlic (minced)
- ➤ ¼ cup of oil (your choice) **(optional)**
- ➤ salt and black pepper to taste

COOKING AND PREPARATION INSTRUCTIONS

STEP 1. In a bowl combine thyme, scallions, onion, allspice, soya sauce, ginger, hoisin sauce, chili-garlic sauce, garlic, oil, salt, and black pepper. Generously brush the sauce on both sides of the steak and refrigerate for 2 hours, or overnight for best results.

STEP 2. Place the steaks in a single layer on a baking pan (on a roasting rack, if possible) and bake in a 350 degree oven for about 5-7 minutes per side, or according to your preference or you can broil the steak.

Serve with any rice dish, steamed callaloo pg 60, sweet potato wedges pg 62, grilled or fried plantain pg 65, and a fresh salad.

Serves 4 people.

OXTAIL STEW

Don't be afraid of oxtail, I say! When prepared properly, the meat is so tender, and this recipe is so delicious. I love oxtail and I find it so hard to understand those who don't like it, especially if they have never tried it. Although time consuming, approximately 3-4½ hours cooking time, as the saying goes, anything good is well worth the wait. I have made oxtail for people who swear they do not like it, but since trying my recipe, they call me to see if oxtail is on the menu, so that they can come over. This is a weekend dish; I usually prepare it on a Sunday around 9:00 a.m. So while the oxtail is cooking away, I have my breakfast and finish up my housework and just relax. By 1:00 p.m. the oxtail is ready and you can enjoy the most delicious and tender oxtail you have ever had. This is pictured on page 82. ♥

- 3½ pounds of oxtail (have your butcher chop into 1-2-inch pieces)
- 3 stalks of scallions (finely chopped)
- 4 tablespoons of dark soya sauce (mushroom flavor)
- 1-2 tablespoons of fresh ginger (finely chopped)
- 6 cloves of garlic (finely chopped)
- 2 teaspoons of allspice
- 1 medium onion (chopped)
- 3 tablespoons of fresh thyme (finely chopped)
- Salt and pepper to taste
- 1 scotch bonnet pepper or any hot pepper (finely chopped) **(optional)**
- 3 to 4 cups water or enough water to cover the meat
- 4 to 5 tablespoons of oil (your choice)
- 1 can of lima beans (19 oz—540 ml)
- 4 tablespoons of cornstarch (if necessary)

COOKING AND PREPARATION INSTRUCTIONS

STEP 1. Wash oxtail well. Add the first 8 ingredients to the oxtail; cover and refrigerate for 2 hours, or overnight for best results.

STEP 2. In a large pot on medium heat, add oil. When oil becomes hot add the meat only **(Remove any large pieces of seasoning from the meat (onion, scallion etc) and reserve)**. Brown meat in batches and put into a large bowl until all meat is browned. Return meat to the pot and add the reserved seasonings and the hot pepper and stir. Add enough water to cover the meat.

STEP 3. Simmer on the stovetop with a tight fitted lid, for 3-4 hours or until the meat is tender. Mix occasionally to avoid sticking. Add the lima beans and continue to cook uncovered on medium heat for about 25-30 minutes, or until liquid in pot reduces and thickens. Stir frequently to avoid any sticking. Using the can of lima beans helps to thicken the sauce.

Serve with rice and peas pg 48 of for dipping those famous festivals pg 20.
Stewing is a slow moist-heat cooking method using a pot with a tight-fitting lid. The meat should be completely covered in liquid. Use for less tender cuts*

Tip: If the liquid is still too watery, add 2-3 tablespoons of cornstarch and mix it with enough water until it has the consistency of heavy cream (smooth). While on medium heat, remove meat from pot. Add flour mixture to the pot slowly until it thickens. Mix well to avoid lumps, and then pour sauce over meat

SPECIAL HUT BURGERS

Everyone loves burgers. Add a few Jamaican spices, however, and you have yourself a mouthwatering delight. This is pictured on pg 83. ♥

- ➢ 1 pound of ground beef
- ➢ ½ cup of onion (finely chopped)
- ➢ 2 stalks of scallions (finely chopped)
- ➢ 2 tablespoons of soya sauce (dark mushroom flavor)
- ➢ 1 teaspoon of allspice
- ➢ 2 teaspoons of fresh ginger (finely chopped)
- ➢ 1 clove of garlic (finely chopped) or 2 teaspoons of garlic powder
- ➢ 1 tablespoon of fresh thyme (finely chopped) or 2 teaspoons ground thyme
- ➢ 1 large egg (beaten)
- ➢ ¼ cup of breadcrumbs
- ➢ salt and black pepper to taste

COOKING AND PREPARATION INSTRUCTIONS

STEP 1.   In a large bowl combine ground beef, onion, scallions, soya sauce, allspice, ginger, garlic, thyme, egg, breadcrumbs, salt, and black pepper; mix well.

STEP 2.   Form into hamburger patties as small or as large as you like.

STEP 3.   Cook until done (bake, broil, grill, and/or fry), 15–25 minutes.

If you like, you can fry the ½ cup of onion, cool, and then add to the mixture; that way the onion is not quite so strong. If you like it hot, you can add your favorite hot sauce or add chopped scotch bonnet pepper to the mix.

Serve with sweet potato wedges pg 62, spiced French fries pg 63, coleslaw pg 53, and top the burger with avocado and tomato salsa pg 15. Another great topping would be grilled onions.

SUBSTITUTE BEEF with ground chicken, turkey, pork, shrimp, and/or a combination of meats.

Serves 4 (easy to double).

CURRY BEEF SHORT RIBS

Beef curry is very popular with the East Indians on the Island, and since my father-in-law's family migrated to Jamaica from East India, I had to add this tasty dish. I Love short ribs and have tones of recipes but I'll save them for another time. Beef short ribs require your love and patience but well worth it... Oh my god! ♥

- ➤ 3½ pounds of short ribs (have the butcher cut in 1" pieces)
- ➤ 3-4 tablespoons of curry powder (preferably a Jamaican—**Grace products**—or Caribbean curry)
- ➤ 3 stalks of scallions (finely chopped)
- ➤ 5 cloves garlic (finely chopped)
- ➤ 2 tablespoons of fresh ginger (finely chopped)
- ➤ 2 tablespoons of fresh thyme (finely chopped)
- ➤ 1 onion (cubed)
- ➤ 1 scotch bonnet or any hot pepper (whole or finely chopped) **(optional)**
- ➤ ¼ cup of Appleton Jamaican Rum
- ➤ 2 cups of water or enough water
- ➤ ¼ cup of oil (your choice)
- ➤ salt and black pepper to taste
- ➤ cornstarch (if necessary)

COOKING AND PREPARATION INSTRUCTIONS

STEP 1. Wash meat. In a large bowl with meat add the curry, scallions, garlic, ginger, thyme, onion, salt, and black pepper; refrigerate up to 2 hours, or for best results, overnight.

STEP 2. In a large pot on medium heat, add oil. When oil becomes hot add the beef short ribs only **(Remove any large pieces of seasoning from the meat (onion, scallion etc) and reserve.** Brown meat in batches and put into a large bowl until all meat is browned. Return meat to the pot and add the rum and cook until most of the liquid evaporates. Then add the reserved seasonings and hot pepper to the meat and mix. Add water, but not directly on the beef.

STEP 3. Simmer on the stovetop with a tight fitted lid, for 1 to 2 hours or until the meat is tender. Continue to cook, uncovered on medium heat for about 20 minutes or until liquid in pot reduces and thickens. Never allow the water to completely absorb, you should always check for enough liquid in the pot.

Tip: If the liquid is still too watery, add 2-3 tablespoons of cornstarch and mix it with enough water until it has the consistency of heavy cream (smooth). While on medium heat, remove meat from pot. Add flour mixture to the pot slowly until it thickens. Mix well to avoid lumps, and then pour sauce over meat

Serve over rice, and or with Roti pg 21.

Serves 4–6 people.

CURRY BEEF WITH ROTI (PG 22)

BASKING IN THE JAMAICAN SUNSHINE IN THE BLUE WATERS
ALWAYS MAKES FOR A RELAXING DAY.

BULLY BEEF FRIED WITH TOMATOES AND ONION

Who would have thought corned beef could be so delicious! Trust me—try this and you will make this part of your meals on the run. Quick meals make for more fun time. ♥

- ➢ 2 cans of corned beef
- ➢ 1 large onion (finely sliced)
- ➢ 2 stalks of scallions (finely chopped)
- ➢ 2 cloves garlic (minced)
- ➢ 1 green pepper (cubed about 1")
- ➢ 1 tablespoon of thyme (finely chopped)
- ➢ 1 scotch bonnet pepper or any hot pepper (finely chopped) **(optional)**
- ➢ 2½ cups of tomatoes (roughly chopped)
- ➢ 1/3 cup of oil (your choice) you can use ¼ cup

COOKING AND PREPARATION INSTRUCTIONS

STEP 1. In a fry pan on medium heat, add oil. When oil becomes hot add the onion, scallions, garlic, green pepper, thyme, and scotch bonnet; sauté for 5 minutes.

STEP 2. Add tomatoes; cook for 4–5 minutes more.

STEP 3. Add corned beef and mix thoroughly, until well heated.

This is traditionally served for breakfast with boiled green banana, boiled dumplings pg 22, or on hardough bread; however, you can enjoy it for any meal. I love to serve with boiled or fried plantains and boiled dumplings. You can add ½ cup of coconut milk in step 3 and cook for a few minutes before adding the corned beef.

Note: Not so traditional, however, you can serve with plain white rice and a fresh salad.

Serves 3–4 people.

FROM TOP LEFT: BEEF PATTIES, BEACH IN OCHO RIOS, ESCOVITCHED FISH, (GRILLED SHRIMP, SEASONED MEATBALLS),JERK PORK, DUNN'S RIVER FALLS, PICK UP SALTFISH WITH FRIED DUMPLINGS AND STIR FRIED SHRIMP. SHOWN BELOW: BEACH IN NEGRIL, SUCH BEAUTY! THIS IS A GREAT PLACE TO ENJOY A COOL DRINK WITH A FESTIVAL.

FROM TOP LEFT: - PUMPKIN SOUP, ACKEE AND SALTFISH WITH BOILED DUMPLINGS AND GREEN BANANA, GRILLED STEAK, OXTAIL, POOL VIEW ON BEAUTIFUL SANDALS DUNN'S RIVER, RED PEA SOUP, PEPPERPOT SOUP, SEAFOOD SALAD, COCONUT CURRY SHRIMP, SPICY CHILI GARLIC STEAK WITH GRILLED PLANTAIN, POTATO SALAD, JAMIN SEASONED CHICKEN, SPICED LEG OF LAMB, HAVING A GOOD TIME ON THE BEACH ONLY IN JAMAICA, CHOCOLATE CHEESCAKE WITH RUM CREAM.

CALLALOO AND CRAB SOUP, OH MY GOODNESS CARROT CAKE, FESTIVALS, CHOCOLATE CAKE, CRAB IN PAPAYA, MOBAY OATMEAL COOKIES, BANANA BREAD, OVEN ROASTED RIBS, SPECIAL HUT BURGER AND SWEET POTATO WEDGES AND MY NIECE ELISABETH HAVING A GREAT TIME ON THE BEAUTIFUL BEACH.

FROM TOP LEFT: GRILLED CHICKEN SANDWICH WITH LIME AND MINT MAYO, BEAUTIFUL JAMAICAN BEACH IS A GREAT PLACE TO RELAX AND UNWIND,COCONUT CHICKEN, CURRY CHICKEN, SUNDAY ROAST CHICKEN, SALMON IN COCONUT CURRY SAUCE, IRIE CHEESECAKE, EXOTIC FRUIT BAKE, MY SISTER-IN-LAW, JODY, READY TO JUMP INTO THE BEAUTIFUL BLUE OCEAN IN NEGRIL, AND SEASONED RICE.

OVEN ROASTED RIBS

This is sure to be a crowd pleaser. So sticky and delicious, so awesome! The flavors explode in your mouth with every bite and you will find it difficult to stop eating. Yet another dish inspired by my father-in-law, Charles. By braising the ribs you will achieve the most tender fall of the bone ribs. So don't blame me when family and friends are a wanting more! This is pictured on pg 83. ♥

- ➤ $\frac{1}{4}$ cup of dark mushroom soya sauce
- ➤ 4–5 cloves of garlic (finely chopped)
- ➤ 2–3 teaspoons of fresh ginger (finely chopped)
- ➤ $\frac{1}{2}$ scotch bonnet pepper or any hot pepper (finely chopped) **(optional)**
- ➤ $\frac{1}{2}$ teaspoon of allspice
- ➤ 1 tablespoon of fresh thyme (finely chopped)
- ➤ 1/3 cup of oil (vegetable/olive)
- ➤ salt and black pepper to taste
- ➤ 2 stalks of small scallions (chopped)
- ➤ $\frac{1}{2}$ cup of hoisin sauce
- ➤ honey to drizzle over ribs
- ➤ 3–4 pounds of pork ribs or baby back ribs (cut the slab in half or in thirds) wash and pat dry

COOKING AND PREPARATION INSTRUCTIONS

STEP 1.   In a large bowl with the ribs add the first 10 ingredients and mix very well. Refrigerate for 2 hours, or overnight, for best results.

STEP 2.   **Cooking method 1-** In a roasting pan, arrange ribs in a single layer and drizzle honey all over ribs. Cover the pan with a tight fitting lid or foil paper to contain steam. **Braise** in the oven (285-300°F) until fork tender around $2\frac{1}{2}$ to 4 hours. Increase temperature to 375 °F and **remove foil and continue to cook the ribs for** an additional 10 minutes per side or until a nice color is achieved- brown and gooey.

STEP 3.   **Cooking method 2** Pre-heat oven to 275 and arrange ribs in a single layer on a cookie sheet and roast slowly for $2\frac{1}{2}$-5 hours or until tender and falls off the bones. Turn ribs over one or two times during cooking, first turn should be around $1\frac{1}{2}$ hours into cooking.

STEP 4.   Once ribs are fork tender brush additional hoisin sauce and drizzle honey all over the ribs, and continue to cook at 370 °F for an additional 10 minutes per side or until a nice color is achieved- brown and gooey on both sides. Remove from pan and cut into smaller pieces and sprinkle with scallions

Serve with potato salad pg 54, coleslaw pg 53 or seasonal vegetables.

Note: Check ribs that are braising after $2\frac{1}{2}$ hours into cooking and continue to cook covered if still not tender. **Be careful when removing foil as the steam is very hot.**

SUBSTITUTE HOISIN SAUCE with barbeque sauce from this book or your favorite.
Serves 4–6 people!

BARBEQUED RIBS

This is my favorite way to make and, of course, eat ribs; so sticky and yummy. Trust me—all will enjoy; a great buffet dish. Your mouth will be dancing with the explosion of flavors; it's fun being adventurous, even if it's only in the kitchen. By braising the ribs which is a slow moist-heat cooking method using a small amount of liquid with a tight-fitting lid you will achieve the most tender fall of the bone ribs. ❤

- ➢ 3 tablespoons of soya sauce
- ➢ 4–6 cloves of garlic (finely chopped)
- ➢ 1 tablespoon of fresh ginger (finely chopped)
- ➢ 1 teaspoon of allspice
- ➢ 1 tablespoon of paprika
- ➢ 1 tablespoon of fresh thyme (finely chopped)
- ➢ 2 stalks of scallions (chopped)
- ➢ ½ scotch bonnet pepper or any hot pepper (finely chopped) **(optional)**
- ➢ ¼ cup of oil (your choice)
- ➢ 1 tablespoon of rum (**Appleton Jamaica Rum** or your choice) **(optional)**
- ➢ ½ cup water
- ➢ salt and black pepper to taste
- ➢ 3–4 pounds of pork ribs or baby back ribs (cut the slab in half or in thirds))
- ➢ 2–3 tablespoons of fresh lime juice
- ➢ ½ cup of hoisin sauce
- ➢ 2 tablespoons of sesame oil

COOKING AND PREPARATION INSTRUCTIONS

STEP 1. In a bowl combine the soya sauce, garlic, ginger, allspice, paprika, thyme, scallions, hot pepper, oil, rum, salt, and black pepper, and mix well. Generously coat the ribs with the mixture and refrigerate for 2 hours, or overnight for best results.

STEP 2. In a roasting pan, arrange ribs in a single layer and cover the pan with a tight fitting lid or foil paper to contain steam. Braise in the oven (280-300°F) until fork tender around 2½ to 4 hours.

STEP 3. In a bowl add hoisin sauce and sesame oil and mix. Turn barbeque on high and grease grill to avoid sticking. Use oil or cooking spray. Place ribs on the hot grill and grill for few minutes per side. Brush sauce onto the ribs and grill on both sides for a few more minute or until gooey. Be very gently as the ribs will be so tender and falling off the bone. Remove from grill cut into smaller pieces and enjoy.

Note: You can add all your ingredients from Step 1 in a food processor and pulse for a few minutes, until a sauce forms. Check ribs that are braising after 2½ hours into cooking and continue to cook covered if still not tender. **Be careful when removing foil as the steam is very hot.**

You can also grill the ribs slowly on low heat hold a temperature around 200 degrees F. **for** 2-4 hours or until tender and falling off the bone.

For In-Direct grilling – You will need 6 cups of wood chips (hickory) - 4 cups of wood chips (hickory) in water and soak for 1 hour and the other 2 cups to be dry.

STEP 1. Build a smoke pouch by squeezing the excess water from the 4 cups of the wet wood chips and place on a large piece of aluminum foil and then place 2 cups of dry wood chips on top of the wet chips and mix them together. Wrap into a square and make sure no chips can fall out.

STEP 2. Using a fork, puncture holes to allow the smoke to flow through and infuse the meat. Remove one side of the grill grate and insert the smoke pouch. Grease grill on both sides to avoid sticking use oil or a cooking spray.

STEP 3. Prepare barbeque for grilling with indirect heat by preheating one side of the grill to 400°F/200°C or high heat and leaving the other side of the grill off. Close lid and wait for smoke.

STEP 4. Place ribs on cool side of grill, opposite from the smoke pouch. Close lid and leave to smoke for $2\frac{1}{2}$-4 hours or until meat is tender and falling off the bone. If you like you can change smoke pouch every 45 minutes. Make 3 or 4 pouches of wood chips as instructed in step 1 and 2.

STEP 5. Remove wood pouch with your tongs. When ribs are cooked move to the side of the grill with the heat and baste with hoisin sauce and grill 2 minutes per side. Remove and enjoy.

SUBSTITUTE HOISIN/SESAME SAUCE with your favorite barbeque sauce. They can be served without any of the sauces; the ribs still taste great.

Serve with potato salad pg 54, grilled corn pg 64, rice, or any of your favorite side dishes.

Serves 4–6 people.

ROAST BEEF

This recipe gives life and zest to the ordinary roast. It's simple and full of flavor. I'm sure you are starting to see a trend with my recipes—Jamaicans like lots of flavor and so do I. Roasting is a dry-heat cooking method used for cooking bigger cuts of beef. No liquid is added or a cover used. This method is used for more tender cuts. This is pictured on the front cover. ♥

- ➤ 1 (4 pound) beef roast rib roast, ribeye roast, tenderloin, tri-tip roast, sirloin roast and rump roast
- ➤ 3 stalks of scallions (chopped)
- ➤ 3 tablespoons of fresh thyme (finely chopped)
- ➤ 6 cloves of garlic (finely chopped)
- ➤ 3 tablespoons of soya sauce
- ➤ 1 tablespoon of allspice
- ➤ 4 tablespoons of rum(**Appleton Jamaica Rum** or your choice) **(optional)**
- ➤ 1 tablespoon of fresh ginger (finely chopped)
- ➤ 1 whole scotch bonnet pepper or any hot pepper (finely chopped) **(optional)**
- ➤ 1/3 of cup oil (your choice) (you can add less $\frac{1}{4}$)
- ➤ salt and black pepper to taste
- ➤ 3 tablespoons of fresh lime juice
- ➤ $\frac{1}{2}$ cup of chicken stock or beef broth
- ➤ $\frac{1}{4}$ cup of wine
- ➤ 2-3 tablespoons of unsalted butter

COOKING AND PREPARATION INSTRUCTIONS

STEP 1.   In a bowl combine scallions, thyme, garlic, soya sauce, allspice, rum, ginger, hot pepper, oil, salt, and pepper, and mix together; pour all over the roast. Refrigerate for 2 hours, or for best results, overnight.

STEP 2.   For more flavor turn stove top to medium. Place a fry pan with some oil. Add the meat to the hot oil and brown meat on all sides. This will help seal the juices (optional). In roasting pan place the beef with the fat side down; add all its marinade, and lime juice. Roast uncovered in a 350 degree, for 1$\frac{1}{2}$ hours or until your desired doneness.

STEP 3.   **For medium-rare,** your meat thermometer should **register 135–140** degrees when inserted in the thickest part of the roast; **for medium**, it should be about **150 degrees.**

STEP 4.   Remove meat from roasting pan and cover with foil and let rest for 15 minutes before cutting. Transfer meat to a plate and pour pan juices or gravy (if using) over the sliced meat.

STEP 5.   For gravy—Place the roasting pan over the stovetop on medium heat, add chicken or beef stock and wine and bring to a boil. Scrape the bottom of the pan with a wooden spoon to release any brown pieces that may be stuck to the pan. Cook on high heat and reduce the liquid by half, stir in butter for richness. To thicken gravy you can add **2-3 tablespoons of cornstarch in a bowl and mix it with enough water until it is smooth. Then** add cornstarch mixture slowly to the gravy and cook on medium heat until gravy thickens. Mix well to avoid lumps, and then pour sauce over meat. This is also great with garlic and thyme sauce (pg 17).

Tip: Roast to desired doneness by removing roast from oven when an oven dial or instant-read meat thermometer inserted in the center of the thickest part of roast reads 10° below final doneness temperature as it will continue to cook with the foil as it's resting(this is called carry over cooking).

Serve with steamed callaloo pg 60 and any rice and peas pg 48 as pictured on the front cover.

Serves 4–6 people

Beef Roasting Guide			
Beef	Weight	Oven Temp.	Cooking Time
Standing Rib Roast	4 to 6 lbs.	325° F	26 to 30 minutes/lb.
Ribeye Roast, boneless	4 to 6 lbs.	350° F	18 to 20 minutes/lb.
Round Tip Roast	4 to 6 lbs.	325° F	25 to 30 minutes/lb.
Tenderloin Roast	4 to 6 lbs.	425° F	45 to 60 minutes total time
Top Loin	4 to 6 lbs.	325° F	17 to 21 minutes/lb.
Strip Loin Roast	6 to 8 lbs.	325° F	14 to 17 mintues/lb.
Top Sirloin Roast	2 to 4 lbs.	350° F	16 to 20 minutes/lb.
Top Round Roast	4 to 6 lbs.	325° F	20 to 25 minutes/lb.
Tri-Tip Roast	1 1/2 to 2 lbs.	425° F	30 to 40 minutes total time
Eye Round Roast	2 to 3 lbs.	325° F	1 1/2 to 1 3/4 hrs. total time

ROAST PORK

This is another dish inspired by my in-laws. I really think this is awesome, the special spices of the Island gives this roast a true cutting edge. In Jamaica they cook most or their roasts on the stovetop; however, I opted for the oven. ♥

- ➢ 1 (3–4 pound) pork loin roast, pork butt or roast of your choice (wash under cold water and pat dry)
- ➢ 3 stalks of scallions (chopped)
- ➢ 2–3 tablespoons of fresh thyme (finely chopped) or 2 teaspoons of ground thyme
- ➢ 2 teaspoons of ground coriander
- ➢ 1 small onion (finely chopped)
- ➢ 6 cloves garlic (finely chopped)
- ➢ 3 tablespoons of soya sauce (dark, preferably mushroom flavor)
- ➢ ¼ cup of hoisin sauce
- ➢ 1½ teaspoons of allspice
- ➢ 1/3 cup of oil (your choice)
- ➢ 2 tablespoons of fresh ginger (finely chopped)
- ➢ 1 scotch bonnet pepper or any hot pepper (finely chopped) **(optional)**
- ➢ salt and black pepper to taste

COOKING AND PREPARATION INSTRUCTIONS

STEP 1. In a bowl add scallions, thyme, onion, garlic, soya sauce, allspice, ground coriander, hoisin sauce, oil, ginger, hot pepper, salt, and black pepper and mix. You can also add the ingredients in a food processor and blend until a thick sauce is achieved. Pour the sauce over the pork, rubbing it all over generously; marinate for 2 hours or overnight.

STEP 2. For more flavor turn stove top to medium. Place a fry pan with some oil. Add the meat to the hot oil and brown meat on all sides. This will help seal the juices (optional). In a roasting pan place the pork with all its marinade, and lime juice. Roast uncovered in a 350 degree, for 1½–2 hours or until your desired doneness.

STEP 3. Baste pork with the pan juices a few times during baking and if at anytime pan juices dry out add some water. When ready a meat thermometer should register between 144-155 degrees when inserted in the thickest part of the roast. You can also insert a fork, and if the juices run clear, it's cooked.

STEP 4. Remove from the oven. Transfer meat to a cutting board, cover with foil, let stand for 10–15 minutes; and then slice. Pour pan juice over meat. To make a thicker sauce pour pan juice in a small pot on medium heat. Add 2 to 3 tablespoons of cornstarch in a bowl and mix it with enough water until it has the consistency of heavy cream (smooth). Add the cornstarch mixture to the pot slowly until it thickens. Mix well to avoid lumps, and then pour sauce over meat.

Tip: Remove roast from the oven when it reads 10° below final doneness temperature as it will continue to cook while covered with the foil as it's resting (this is called carry over cooking).

Serve with any rice dish, potato salad pg 54 or coleslaw 53. If you are really short on time, I find frozen corn to be a signature twist of mine to most of the recipes in this book.

ROAST PORK

THE BOYS ENJOYING A NICE DAY OUT! SHOWN HERE IS MY SON
ANDREW WITH MY NEPHEWS SAM AND NICOLAS.

GRILLED BONELESS PORK ROAST

As I mentioned earlier in this book, I love the marrying of fruit with savory foods, and this is another great example of how great it tastes. ♥

- 1 (3–4 pounds) boneless pork loin roast or pork of your choice (wash and pat dry)
- 5 cloves of garlic
- 2 stalks of scallions (roughly chopped)
- 1½ tablespoons of fresh ginger (roughly chopped)
- 1/3 cup of hoisin sauce
- 1 cup of fresh ripe mango (roughly chopped)
- 1 small onion (roughly chopped)
- 1 tablespoon of fresh thyme (chopped)
- 1 tablespoon of soya sauce (dark, preferably mushroom flavor)
- ¼ cup of oil (your choice)
- 3 tablespoons of lime juice
- 1 scotch bonnet pepper or any hot pepper (chopped) **(optional)**
- salt and black pepper
- 1 cup of water

COOKING AND PREPARATION INSTRUCTIONS

STEP 1. In a blender or food processor add the garlic, scallions, ginger, hoisin sauce, mango, onion, thyme, soya sauce, oil, lime juice, hot pepper, salt, and black pepper. Blend until a smooth sauce is achieved.

STEP 2. In bowl place pork roast and poke holes throughout meat and add ½ of the sauce and rub all over the meat. Refrigerate 2–3 hours, or overnight for best results.

STEP 3. In a small pot on medium heat cook the other half of the sauce with 1 cup of water for 35–40 minutes, or until thick, stirring frequently toward the end. Cool and refrigerate for later use.

STEP 4. Make sure to grease the grill to avoid sticking. Heat one side of the barbeque on high the other side should not be turned on. (This is called indirect cooking).

STEP 5. Place a drip pan on the side of the grill that has no heat to catch any dripping of the pork. First place the pork directly on the side of the grill that is heated and sear on all sides. Then transfer pork on the side of the grill that has no heat.

STEP 6. Grill with the lid closed for 1½ –4 hours, or until the thermometer, inserted into the thickest part of the pork, reads between 145-155degrees. Be sure to occasionally baste the pork with the sauce from **Step 3**. If you are not comfortable unless your pork is cooked until it reaches 160 degree please feel free to serve it to your guests that way. It will not be as moist. No problems mon! You're the boss.

STEP 7. Remove from grill and place in a baking dish and cover with foil; let stand for 10-15 minutes, and then slice. Pork should be cooked 20–25 minutes per pound!

Great side dishes are rice and peas pg 48, potato salad 54, and steamed calalloo pg 60 .
Serve with mango salsa pg 15.

Serves 4 people.

GRILLED PORK TENDERLION WITH SPICY MANGO SAUCE

This is definitely a crowd favorite. Again, the marrying of sweet with heat is a perfect blend of taste explosion in one's mouth. This serves 3–4 people with a side dish. ❤

- ➢ 3 (1-pound) pork tenderloins silver skin removed.
- ➢ 5 cloves of garlic (finely chopped)
- ➢ 2 tablespoons of fresh thyme and mint (finely chopped)
- ➢ 1 teaspoon each of **allspice** and **paprika**
- ➢ 1 tablespoon of fresh ginger (finely chopped)
- ➢ 1/3 cup of oil (olive; however, you can use any type you like)
- ➢ 2 tablespoons each of fresh **lime juice** and **soya sauce**
- ➢ 1½ tablespoons of brown sugar
- ➢ salt and black pepper to taste
- ➢ **SPICY MANGO SAUCE**
- ➢ 1 cup of mango (partially ripe to ripe, chopped)
- ➢ 2 teaspoons of brown sugar
- ➢ 1 teaspoon of fresh ginger (finely chopped)
- ➢ 1 clove of garlic (finely chopped)
- ➢ 5 teaspoons of crushed red pepper sauce (**Grace products** or your choice)
- ➢ ½ scotch bonnet pepper or any hot pepper (finely chopped) (if you want it really hot use 1 pepper)
- ➢ ¼ cup of oil (your choice)
- ➢ 4 tablespoons each of **fresh lime juice** and **vinegar**
- ➢ salt and black pepper
- ➢ 1 cup water

COOKING AND PREPARATION INSTRUCTIONS

STEP 1. Wash pork; set aside. In a bowl add garlic, thyme, allspice, paprika, ginger, oil, lime juice, soya sauce, brown sugar, salt, and black pepper, and mix gently. Place pork in a bowl or re-sealable bag, add the marinade, and coat the meat well; refrigerate for 2 hours or overnight.

STEP 2. For spicy mango sauce, add the mango, brown sugar, ginger, garlic, red pepper sauce, hot pepper, oil, lime juice, vinegar, salt, and black pepper into a food processor and mix to form a sauce. In a small pot add the sauce and the water and cook over medium to low heat for 25–40 minutes or until sauce is thickened. Allow to cool. You can serve sauce at room temperature, or refrigerator until ready to use. Can be kept in fridge for 3–4 days. Preheat barbeque to high and make sure to grease the grill to avoid sticking.

STEP 3. Grill tenderloin on high heat; sear each side. Continue to cook on medium heat with the lid closed for 12–15 minutes, or until the thermometer, when inserted into the thickest part of the tenderloin, reads between 140-155 degrees. Be sure to turn meat several times during cooking. Remove from grill, place into baking dish, cover with foil, and let stand for 10–15 minutes. Slice meat on a diagonal and arrange on a platter.

Drizzle generously the spicy mango sauce over the sliced meat. Or you can serve the mango salsa pg 15. Serve with any rice dish, sweet potato wedges pg 62, grilled corn 64, or plantains pg 65.

SPICED LEG OF LAMB

This is amazing! If you like lamb, you will be in heaven! The spices marry so well with the lamb and it makes this a mouthwatering dish. This is pictured on pg 82. ♥

- 1 (4-5-pound) leg of lamb
- 4 stalks scallions (chopped)
- 3 tablespoons of fresh thyme (finely chopped)
- 7 cloves of garlic (finely chopped)
- 3 tablespoons of soya sauce (dark, mushroom flavor)
- 2 teaspoons of allspice
- 1 teaspoon of cinnamon
- 4 tablespoons of rum (**Appleton Jamaica Rum** or your choice) **(optional)**
- 1 tablespoon of fresh ginger (finely chopped)
- 1 scotch bonnet pepper (chopped) or any hot pepper (finely chopped) **(optional)**
- 1/3 cup of oil (your choice) (you can use less ¼; it will work okay)
- 3 tablespoons of fresh lime juice
- salt and black pepper to taste

COOKING AND PREPARATION INSTRUCTIONS

STEP 1. Wash leg of lamb well and pat dry; set aside in a big bowl.

STEP 2. In a small bowl add the scallions, thyme, garlic, soya sauce, allspice, cinnamon, rum, ginger, hot pepper, oil, lime juice, salt, and black pepper, and mix together, or you can add all the ingredients directly over the lamb.

STEP 3. Spread sauce all over the lamb generously and marinate for 3 hours, or for best results, overnight.

STEP 4. Add leg of lamb to a roasting pan with all the juices from the marinade. Pace the leg of lamb on in a roasting pan. Preheat oven to 375 degrees.

STEP 5. Roast leg of lamb uncovered and baste with the pan juices a few times during baking. About halfway into cooking, check to see if the pan juices have dried out: and if so add ¼ cup water. If at any time the lamb is over-browning cover with foil. For rare the temperature should register 135 degree, medium-rare your meat thermometer should register about 145-150 degrees and for well done the meat thermometer should register about 160-170 degrees when inserted into the thickest part of the roast; or cook to your preference.

STEP 6. Remove from heat and reserve juices. Cover with foil and let rest for 10–15 minutes. Slice and pour juice (gravy) over the meat. A great choice for a sauce is the garlic and thyme sauce. To make a quick gravy see Roast beef recipe (pg 88).

Serve with rice and peas pg 48, steamed calalloo pg 60, Island love mashed sweet potato 6, and sweet potato wedges pg 62.

Serves 4-6 people

CURRY GOAT

Even if you don't like goat, I dare you to make it, because you'll like it prepared this way. Give it a try—it's amazing. Did you know that goat is low in fat? Isn't that enough to make you try it? Most people add potato, but I don't in my recipe, because I usually make potato salad as my side dish with this one. ♥

- ➢ 3½-4 pounds of goat (cut into small pieces, 2 inch; ask your butcher) (wash well)
- ➢ ¼-1/3 cup Appleton Jamaican Rum (optional)
- ➢ 3 stalks of scallions (finely chopped)
- ➢ 2–3 tablespoons of fresh thyme (finely chopped)
- ➢ 1 large onion (chopped into cubes)
- ➢ 6 cloves of garlic (finely chopped)
- ➢ 3–4 tablespoons of curry powder (preferably a Jamaican—**Grace products**—or Caribbean curry)
- ➢ 1 tablespoon of fresh ginger (finely chopped)
- ➢ 1 scotch bonnet pepper or any hot pepper (whole or chopped) **(optional)**
- ➢ salt and black pepper
- ➢ 3 tablespoons of oil (your choice)
- ➢ 2 cups of water + (more water if necessary)
- ➢ cornstarch

COOKING AND PREPARATION INSTRUCTIONS

STEP 1. In a large bowl with the goat combine the scallions, thyme, onion, garlic, curry powder, ginger, hot pepper, salt, and black pepper; mix well. Marinate for 2 hours, or preferably overnight.

STEP 2. In a large pot on medium heat, add oil. When oil becomes hot add the goat meat only **(Remove any large pieces of seasoning from the meat (onion, scallion etc) and reserve.** Brown meat in batches and add to a large bowl until all meat is all browned.

STEP 3. Return meat to the pot and add the rum and cook until most of the liquid evaporates. Add the seasonings from step 2, and stir everything together and then add the water.

STEP 4. Cook on low (simmer), covered, for 2–4 hours, or until meat is fork tender, stirring occasionally add more water if necessary.

STEP 5. Continue to cook on medium heat, uncovered, for about 15-20 minutes more or until liquid in pot reduces and thickens. Never allow the liquid to completely absorb, always check for enough liquid in the pot. If you like more gravy then you can add more water and bring to a boil. Remove from heat.

Tip: If the liquid is still too watery, add 2-3 tablespoons of cornstarch and mix it with enough water until it has the consistency of heavy cream (smooth). While on medium heat, remove meat from pot. Add flour mixture to the pot slowly until it thickens. Mix well to avoid lumps, and then pour sauce over meat

Serve with roti pg 21, potato salad pg 54, or a rice dish.
I like adding the Rum because not only does it add flavor but it also helps tenderize the meat. And also any excuse to get the Rum out makes me happy! You can also find ready chopped stewing goat meat in the frozen sections of most grocery stores throughout North America and in West Indian Stores.

Serves 4-6 people

CURRY CHICKEN

Chicken is a good way to introduce oneself and others to curry. Try this recipe and you will be pleasantly surprised by how good it is. This recipe is handed down to me from my mother-in-law, Marcia. In Jamaican cooking, it is wise to use Caribbean or, preferably, Jamaican curry. For first time curry users, it's a milder version than the Indian curry. This is pictured on cover the front cover. ♥

- 12 pieces of chicken legs or thighs (cut chicken pieces in half or in quarters for quicker cooking.)
- 3 stalks of scallions (finely chopped)
- 2–3 tablespoons of fresh thyme (finely chopped)
- 1 large onion chopped
- 5 cloves of garlic (finely chopped)
- 3–4 tablespoons of curry powder (preferably a Jamaican—Grace products—or Caribbean curry)
- 1 tablespoon of fresh ginger (finely chopped)
- 1 scotch bonnet pepper or any hot pepper (finely chopped) **(optional)**
- salt and black pepper
- 3 tablespoons of oil (your choice)
- ½ cup of water **(optional)**
- cornstarch (if necessary)

COOKING AND PREPARATION INSTRUCTIONS

STEP 1. Wash chicken with cold water. In a large bowl with the chicken combine the scallions, thyme, onion, garlic, curry powder, ginger, hot pepper, salt, and black pepper; mix well. Marinate for 2 hours, or preferably overnight.

STEP 2. In a large pot on medium heat add oil. When oil becomes hot add chicken only **(Remove any large pieces of seasoning from the meat (onion, scallion etc) and reserve**. Brown meat in batches and add to a large bowl until all meat is all browned. Once the chicken is browned add it back to the pot with the seasonings and stir everything together.

STEP 3. Cook on low to medium heat, covered, for approximately 40–50 minutes, or until chicken is cooked. Mix frequently to avoid sticking and drying out, if necessary add some water.

STEP 4. Continue to cook chicken uncovered for an additional 5 more minutes, stir frequently. Chicken is done when the juice run clear when pricked with a fork.

STEP 5. **Optional**- For more gravy, remove cooked chicken from pot; add ½ cup of water and cook uncovered for 10 minutes or until liquid thickens and return chicken to pot. The gravy should not be watery.

Tip: If the liquid is still too watery, add 2-3 tablespoons of cornstarch and mix it with enough water until it has the consistency of heavy cream (smooth). While on medium heat, remove meat from pot. Add flour mixture to the pot slowly until it thickens. Mix well to avoid lumps, and then pour sauce over meat

Note: Most Jamaican's I know do not add water at all; however, I like extra gravy to pour over rice.

Serve with roti pg 21 and/or with any rice dish. Potato salad pg 54 is also an excellent accompaniment.

Serves 4–6 people.

CARIBBEAN BREADED CHICKEN

This is truly a huge hit with the kids and the adults too. Can't make enough and there is usually no left over. That might have something to do that we love to eat never get enough!! Try this and you will make this all the time. Cheers! ♥

- 12-14 pieces of boneless skinless chicken thighs- regular chicken thighs or legs are fine
- 1½ cup of plain breadcrumbs
- ½ cup corn meal + more if necessary
- 2 eggs beaten
- 1/3 cup water
- 3 teaspoons of allspice
- 2 teaspoons of paprika
- 1½-2 tablespoons garlic powder
- 1 teaspoon of ground coriander
- ground thyme
- 2 tablespoon of fresh cilantro finely minced
- 2 tablespoons of soya sauce
- Salt and black pepper to taste

STEP 1. Wash chicken with cold water. In al large bowl with the chicken add the soya sauce, salt and pepper. Set aside

STEP 2. In a bowl add the eggs and water; mix well. On a large piece of parchment paper or large shallow dish add the corn meal and in another large piece of parchment paper or large shallow dish add the breadcrumbs. To the bread crumbs add the allspice, paprika, garlic powder, ground coriander, ground thyme, pinch of salt, black pepper and fresh cilantro and mix to combine.

STEP 3. Dip each chicken piece into the corn meal, then the egg mixture and finally into the breadcrumbs. Make sure to cover each piece of chicken.

STEP 4. On a large cookie sheet with parchment paper brush generously with oil. Place each piece of chicken in a single layer on the cookie sheet and bake at 350 degrees for about 20-25 minutes. Turn chicken after 15 minutes so both sides get a nice golden color. Chicken is done when the juice run clear when pricked with a fork about 45 minutes.

Discard any left over breadcrumbs, corn meal and the egg.

If using regular chicken thighs or legs increase cooking time.

Great sauce is the fresh garlic and thyme sauce pg 17, tomato chutney pg 14 or fresh citrus sauce pg 16. Serve with rice and pea's pg 48, potato salad pg 54, coleslaw pg 53.

Serves 6 people

OVEN BARBEQUED CHICKEN WINGS

If you like chicken wings, go no further. Run to your nearest grocery store, buy some wings, and make one of the best wings ever. You will thank me. ❤

- $3\frac{1}{2}$ pounds of chicken wings (wash wings with cold water)
- 3 tablespoons of soya sauce
- 3-4 teaspoons of ground garlic powder
- 4 teaspoons of paprika
- 2 teaspoons of ground thyme
- 2 teaspoons of allspice
- 1 teaspoon of cumin
- 3 stalks of scallions (finely chopped)
- 1 tablespoon of fresh ginger (finely chopped)
- salt and black pepper to taste
- 1/3 cup oil (your choice) you can use $\frac{1}{4}$ if you are watching your fat intake
- 1 scotch bonnet pepper or any hot pepper (finely chopped) **(optional)**
- barbeque sauce below, your favorite prepared barbeque sauce, or hoisin sauce

COOKING AND PREPARATION INSTRUCTIONS

STEP 1. In a bowl combine oil, garlic, soya sauce, paprika, thyme, allspice, cumin, scallions, ginger, salt, black pepper, oil, and hot pepper, and mix together; set aside. In a large bowl with the wings pour the sauce all over generously and mix very well. Marinate in refrigerator for 2 hours, or overnight for best results.

STEP 2. Preheat oven to 350 degrees. Place wings in a single layer on a baking pan (on a roasting rack, if possible) and bake for 35–55 minutes until golden and fully cooked. Turn chicken wings over one time during baking.

STEP 3. Add barbeque sauce from below or your favorite and cook 5–7 minutes on each side (broil if you can).

BARBEQUE SAUCE
- $\frac{1}{2}$ cup of ketchup
- 1/3 cup of hoisin sauce
- $\frac{1}{4}$ cup of vinegar
- 3 cloves of garlic (finely chopped)
- 1 tablespoon of fresh ginger (finely chopped)
- 2 teaspoons of ground thyme
- 2 teaspoons of cumin
- 2 tablespoons of rum (**Appleton Jamaica Rum** or your choice)
- 1 teaspoon of ground garlic powder
- $\frac{1}{4}$ cup of oil (your choice)
- $1\frac{1}{2}$ cups of water

COOKING AND PREPARATION INSTRUCTIONS

STEP 1. In a small pot on medium heat, add oil, garlic, and ginger, and cook for 1–2 minutes. Remove from heat and add ketchup, hoisin sauce, vinegar, rum, dried thyme, cumin, and garlic powder; mix well and add water and return pot to medium heat. Continue to cook on medium heat for about 40–50 minutes, until thick, mixing constantly toward the end. Once the sauce is cooled, remove the extra oil on the surface.

This is also a favorite with kids; just omit scotch bonnet pepper.

SUBSTITUTE BARBEQUE SAUCE with honey or hoisin sauce with sesame oil.

SUBSTITUTE RUB
- $1\frac{1}{2}$ tablespoons each of **paprika, allspice, cumin, garlic powder,** and **cayenne pepper**
- 2 teaspoons of brown sugar
- 1 teaspoon of dried thyme and **cinnamon**
- 1/3 cup of oil
- 1 tablespoon of ginger (finely chopped)
- salt and black pepper to taste

SEE ABOVE FOR COOKING AND PREPARATION INSTRUCTIONS ON PAGE 114.

This rub would be great with ribs. Use $3\frac{1}{2}$ pounds and brush with barbeque sauce; same as in chicken recipe.

Serves 4 people.

YUMMY CHICKEN WINGS

GRILLED CHICKEN WITH PINEAPPLE KEBOBS

I have to tell you, this is so good! I really can't express it more than that; you'll just have to make and try them to understand. The flavors work so well; they are fresh, and you will feel like you are on an island in the Caribbean, like Jamaica. ❤

- ➢ 3 pounds of chicken breasts (cubed into2-inch pieces) (wash chicken with cold water)
- ➢ 3 stalks of scallions (finely chopped)
- ➢ 1 teaspoon of allspice
- ➢ 2 tablespoons of dark soya sauce (mushroom flavored)
- ➢ 1–2 tablespoons of fresh thyme (finely chopped) or 1 teaspoon of dried thyme
- ➢ salt and black pepper to taste
- ➢ 1/3 cup oil (your choice)
- ➢ 4 cloves garlic (finely chopped)
- ➢ 2 green peppers (chopped into cubes)
- ➢ 1 large onion (chopped into cubes)
- ➢ 2 cups of pineapple (chopped into cubes)
- ➢ 1/3 cup honey
- ➢ 4 tablespoons of fresh lime juice
- ➢ 1 tablespoon of fresh mint (finely chopped)
- ➢ 1 tablespoon of crushed red pepper sauce or garlic chili paste(**Grace products** or your choice)
- ➢ 8-10 skewers (If using wooden skewers –soak skewers in water to avoid burning)

COOKING AND PREPARATION INSTRUCTIONS

STEP 1.   In a bowl combine the scallions, allspice, soya sauce, thyme, salt, black pepper, oil, and garlic, and mix together. Pour sauce all over the chicken along with the peppers and onion and combine well. Marinate for 2 hours, or overnight for best results.

STEP 2.   Peel and cut pineapple into 2-inch cubes and refrigerate until ready to use.

STEP 3.   Arrange cubed chicken alternately with cubed pepper, pineapple, and onion on a skewer. Preheat barbeque to medium and make sure to grease the grill to avoid sticking. You can use oil or a cooking spray.

STEP 4.   Close lid and grill chicken skewers until done, about 5-7 minutes per side.

STEP 5.   In the meantime, combine in a small bowl the honey, lime juice, mint, and hot pepper. Brush the sauce on the grilled chicken. Grill each side for one more. Remove from grill.

Plate and top with chopped fresh mint.

Enjoy with any rice dish, coleslaw pg 53, potato salad pg 54, or any side dish of your choice.

Serves 4 people.

GRILLED CHICKEN WITH PINEAPPLE

ME WITH MY JAMAICAN-ITALIAN PRINCE

BARBEQUED CHICKEN

I love this dish. Nothing tastes better than grilled food. Trust me, this is so mouthwatering, you will be making this all summer long, and if you are lucky enough to live in sunshine year round, well, then you can enjoy this all the time. I'm jealous. ♥

- 10–12 pieces of chicken thighs or drumsticks (wash chicken with cold water)
- 3 stalks of scallions (finely chopped)
- 2 tablespoons of fresh thyme (finely chopped) or 2 teaspoons of ground thyme
- 3 teaspoons of allspice
- 5 cloves of garlic (finely chopped)
- 1 teaspoon of cinnamon
- 2 teaspoons of brown sugar
- 3 teaspoons of paprika
- 2–3 tablespoons of soya sauce (dark, mushroom flavor)
- 1 tablespoon of fresh ginger (finely chopped)
- 1 scotch bonnet pepper or any hot pepper (finely chopped) **(optional)**
- 1/3 cup of oil (your choice)
- salt and black pepper to taste
- 2 tablespoons of fresh lime juice
- ½–1 cup of barbeque sauce (your favorite)

COOKING AND PREPARATION INSTRUCTIONS

STEP 1. In a large bowl combine the scallions, thyme, allspice, garlic, cinnamon, brown sugar, paprika, soya sauce, ginger, hot pepper, oil, salt, and black pepper; mix well. Pour sauce over the chicken, coating very well. Marinate in refrigerator for 2 hours, or overnight for best results.

STEP 2. Preheat barbeque to medium and make sure to grease the grill to avoid sticking.

STEP 3. Remove chicken from fridge and add the lime juice. Close lid and grill chicken until done, about 15–25 minutes, turning chicken occasionally. Chicken is done when the juice run clear when pricked with a fork.

STEP 4. Brush barbeque sauce on chicken and grill each side for an additional 2–3 minutes.

SUBSTITUTE BARBEQUE SAUCE with hoisin sauce.

You can omit sauces and enjoy as is.

Serve with any rice dishes in this book, grilled plantain pg 65 fresh garlic and thyme sauce pg 17, and a fresh salad.

There you have it, another quick meal!

Serves 4–6 people.

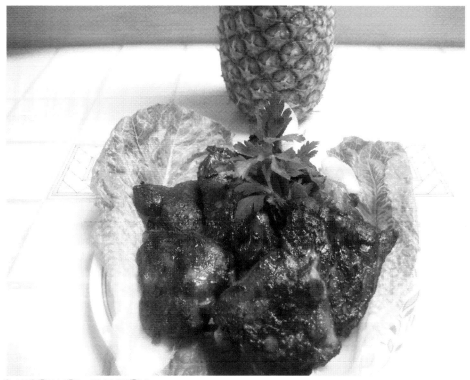

BARBEQUED CHICKEN

THERE IS ALWAYS TIME FOR SHOPPING. YOU NEVER KNOW WHAT
YOU MIGHT FIND BY THE ROADSIDE—ONLY IN JAMAICA. HAPPY
 SHOPPING, GIRLS, AND YOU TOO, BOYS!

JAMIN' SEASONED CHICKEN

This will quickly become one of your favorite recipes, and your kids will love it too. Again, this recipe was inspired by Marcia (my mother-in-law), so I hope this tasty chicken dish will grace your tables very soon. This is pictured on pg 82. ♥

- ➢ 10–12 pieces of chicken thighs or drumsticks (wash chicken)
- ➢ 1 green pepper (cut into cubes)
- ➢ 1 large onion (sliced)
- ➢ 2 stalks of scallions (roughly chopped)
- ➢ 2–3 tablespoons of fresh thyme (finely chopped)
- ➢ 2 teaspoons of allspice
- ➢ 1 tablespoon of paprika
- ➢ 7 cloves of garlic (finely chopped)
- ➢ 3 tablespoons of soya sauce (preferably dark, mushroom flavor)
- ➢ 2 teaspoons of fresh ginger (finely chopped)
- ➢ 1 scotch bonnet pepper or any hot pepper (finely chopped) (optional)
- ➢ 1/3 cup of oil (your choice)
- ➢ salt and black pepper to taste
- ➢ ½–1 cup of barbeque sauce or enough to cover chicken (your favorite, or from pages 114 and 115)

COOKING AND PREPARATION INSTRUCTIONS

STEP 1. In a bowl with the chicken, peppers, and onion, add the scallions, thyme, garlic, soya sauce, ginger, paprika, hot pepper, oil, salt, and black pepper; mix well. Marinate in refrigerate for 2 hours, or overnight for best results.

STEP 2. Transfer chicken to a roasting pan and cook covered for 20minutes.

STEP 3. Continue to cook uncovered for 25 minutes more, or until fully cooked.

STEP 4. Add barbeque sauce on each piece of chicken and bake for an additional 5 minutes per side, or you can broil. Chicken is done when the juice run clear when pricked with a fork.

Remove from oven and serve.

Serve with any rice dish, potato salad pg 54, coleslaw pg 53 or a fresh salad.

You can omit the barbeque sauce and it will taste equally as good.

If serving to children, make sure to add barbeque sauce they love it. My son requests this almost every day and I don't blame him—I love it too.

For more gravy I like to add 1 cup of water in step 2, remember not to add water directly on chicken. Kids seem to love gravy over the rice and on their chicken too.

Serves 4–6 people.

COCONUT CHICKEN

The coconut milk infused with garlic, ginger, and thyme really makes for a tasty meal that you won't soon forget and it will make you long for more. I enjoyed this several times at Nanny's house and each time I make it, the incredible smell is a joyful reminder of her. This is pictured on pg 84. ♥

- ➢ 3 pounds of chicken breast (washed, pound chicken so it's even and sliced 1" thick)
- ➢ 1 cup of tomato's (chopped)
- ➢ $1\frac{1}{4}$ cups of coconut milk (**Grace product** or your choice)
- ➢ $\frac{1}{2}$ cup of water
- ➢ 1 small onion (chopped)
- ➢ 3 stalks of scallions (finely chopped)
- ➢ 3 cloves of garlic (finely chopped)
- ➢ 2 teaspoons of fresh ginger (finely chopped)
- ➢ 1–2 tablespoons of fresh thyme (finely chopped)
- ➢ 1 scotch bonnet pepper or any hot pepper (finely chopped) **(optional)**
- ➢ salt and black pepper to taste
- ➢ cornstarch

COOKING AND PREPARATION INSTRUCTIONS

STEP 1. Turn the heat to medium. Place fry pan on heat and add oil. Add onion, scallions, garlic, ginger, thyme, and hot pepper to the hot oil and sauté for a few minutes. In a bowl add coconut milk, water and 2 tablespoons of cornstarch and mix well to avoid lumps, you can use a whisk to help you out. Add the mixture to the pan and cook on low heat for about 20-25 minutes, or until it reduces to half and thickens. Stir often.

STEP 2. Add chicken, salt, black pepper, and tomato to pan and give a good stir. Cook chicken covered for 10 minutes or until chicken is fully cooked. You should end up with a nice sauce to pour over rice. If necessary add more water.

Tip: If the liquid is still too watery, add 2-3 tablespoons of cornstarch and mix it with enough water until it has the consistency of heavy cream (smooth). While on medium heat, remove meat from pot. Add flour mixture to the pot slowly until it thickens. Mix well to avoid lumps, and then pour sauce over meat

Serve hot over rice.

SUBSTITUTE CHICKEN with lobster meat, crabmeat, shrimp, or salmon

Serves 4 people

CITRUS OVEN BAKED CHICKEN

Chicken prepared this way brings me right back to Jamaica (the rum, the lime, the oranges); it's refreshing, like jumping into a pool or the ocean. To be in Jamaica right about know! ♥

- ➢ 1 (4–5-pound) roasting chicken
- ➢ salt and black pepper to taste
- ➢ 1/3 cup of oil (your choice)
- ➢ ¼ cup each of lime juice and orange juice
- ➢ ½ teaspoon of each of lime and orange zest
- ➢ 4 cloves of garlic (finely chopped) + 3 whole cloves garlic (for cavity)
- ➢ 1 tablespoon of fresh ginger (finely chopped)
- ➢ 3 stalks of scallions (chopped)
- ➢ 3 tablespoons of rum **(optional)** (**Appleton Jamaica Rum** or your choice)
- ➢ 3 tablespoons of soya sauce (preferably dark, mushroom flavor)
- ➢ 1 teaspoon of allspice
- ➢ 2–3 tablespoons of fresh thyme (finely chopped)
- ➢ 1 scotch bonnet pepper or any hot pepper (finely chopped) **(optional)**

COOKING AND PREPARATION INSTRUCTIONS

STEP 1. Wash chicken and **tie the legs with butcher string (optional).** In a large bowl season chicken with salt and pepper.

STEP 2. In a small bowl whisk oil, lime juice, orange juice, lime zest, orange zest, then add chopped garlic, ginger, scallions, rum, soya sauce, allspice, thyme, and scotch bonnet; mix well.

STEP 3. In a large bowl with the chicken, pour the sauce all over generously, including in the cavity. Add the whole cloves of garlic into the cavity and marinate in refrigerator for 2 hours, or overnight for best results.

STEP 4. Preheat oven to 370 degree and transfer chicken to a roasting pan (on a roasting rack, if possible).

STEP 5. Roast for approximately 1-2 hours uncovered until chicken is cooked. Baste with juices several times during roasting. When chicken is cooked the legs and wings pull away from chicken, or when a fork is inserted the juices run clear. When fully cooked a meat thermometer should register 180 degrees when inserted into the thickest part of the thigh.

STEP 6. Reserve pan juices and transfer chicken to a cutting board, cover with foil and allow to rest for 10 minutes before carving. Pour pan juices or gravy (optional) over the sliced chicken. To make a quick gravy see Roast beef recipe pg 88.

This is so refreshing and delicious; it will transport you to a tropical island like Jamaica.

Serve with any rice dish, potato salad pg 54, fresh garlic and thyme sauce pg 17, and a nice, cold tropical drink. **Everyting cool, mon.**
Serves 4–6 people.

SUNDAY BAKED CHICKEN

This is a nice Sunday dish, inspired by Auntie Sanny, who lives in Spanish Town. I can't tell you enough how much I love this. The taste explodes in your mouth with so many flavors, you just have to make it and try it for yourself to understand. This is a hit with the kids. ♥

- 1 (4–5-pound) roasting chicken
- 3 stalks of scallions (chopped)
- salt and black pepper to taste
- 2–3 tablespoons of fresh thyme (finely crushed)
- 5 cloves of garlic (finely crushed) + 3 whole cloves garlic (for cavity)
- 1½ teaspoons of allspice
- 3 tablespoons of soya sauce (preferably dark, mushroom flavor)
- ½ cup of hoisin sauce (make sure to cover the chicken generously)
- 1 tablespoon of fresh ginger (finely crushed)
- 1 scotch bonnet pepper or any hot pepper (finely crushed) **(optional)**
- 1/3 cup of oil (your choice) or you can use ¼ cup

COOKING AND PREPARATION INSTRUCTIONS

STEP 1. Wash chicken and pat dry and **tie the legs with butcher string (optional)**. In a small bowl add the scallions, salt, black pepper, thyme, garlic, allspice, soya sauce, hoisin sauce, ginger, hot pepper, and oil; mix together.

STEP 2. In a large bowl with the chicken, pour the sauce all over generously, including in the cavity. Add the whole cloves of garlic into the cavity and marinate in refrigerator for 2 hours, or overnight for best results.

STEP 3. Preheat oven to 350 degrees. Transfer the chicken to a roasting pan (on a roasting rack, if possible) and pour marinade directly on chicken.

STEP 4. Roast uncovered for 1½-2 hours until cooked and golden. Baste with pan juices several times during roasting. When chicken is cooked the legs and wings pull away from the chicken, or when a fork is inserted the juices run clear. When fully cooked a meat thermometer should register 180 degrees when inserted into the thickest part of the thigh.

STEP 5. Reserve pan juices and transfer chicken to a cutting board, cover with foil and allow to rest for 10 minutes before carving. Pour pan juices over the cut chicken.

This gives new meaning to delicious. Trust me, all will love it.

Serve with any rice dish, coleslaw salad pg 53, or potato salad pg 54.

Serve with Island love mashed sweet potatoes pg 62 for a formal affair.

Serves 4–6 people.

STEWED CHICKEN/FRICASEE

This is another dish that I learned from my father-in-law. Man, can he cook! I love the fusion of cultures in the food, because it really has made Jamaican food exciting, as are its people. ❤

- ➢ 12 pieces of chicken thighs or drumsticks (wash with cold water)
- ➢ 2 cups of chopped carrots cut into 2 inch pieces
- ➢ 3 tablespoons of oil (your choice)
- ➢ 3 stalks of scallions (chopped)
- ➢ 4 cloves of garlic (finely chopped)
- ➢ 1 medium onion (cubed)
- ➢ 2 teaspoons of fresh ginger (finely chopped)
- ➢ 1 scotch bonnet pepper or any hot pepper (finely chopped) **(optional)**
- ➢ 2–3 tablespoons of fresh thyme (finely chopped)
- ➢ 3 teaspoons of paprika
- ➢ 2 teaspoons of allspice
- ➢ 3 tablespoons of soya sauce (preferably dark, mushroom flavor)
- ➢ salt and black pepper
- ➢ 2 cups of water + (more water if necessary)
- ➢ boiled dumplings (page 22) (shape as spinners)
- ➢ cornstarch

COOKING AND PREPARATION INSTRUCTIONS

STEP 1. Prepare your dumplings (see page 22). For this recipe, shape dumplings into small saucer shapes or spinners.

STEP 2. Turn the heat to medium. Place fry pan on heat and add the oil. Add the scallions, garlic, onion, ginger, and scotch bonnet pepper to the hot oil and sauté for 5 minutes.

STEP 3. Add the chicken and brown on each side. Add the thyme, paprika, allspice, soya sauce, salt, and black pepper stir well. Add the carrots and water. Finally add the dumpling right on the top and cook covered on medium heat, for approximately 35-45 minutes or until chicken is cooked. Mix occasionally to avoid sticking. The steam in the pot will cook the dumplings.

STEP 4. Cook uncovered for a few minutes to thicken the sauce.

Tip: If the liquid is still too watery, add 2-3 tablespoons of cornstarch and mix it with enough water until it has the consistency of heavy cream (smooth). While on medium heat, remove meat from pot. Add flour mixture to the pot slowly until it thickens. Mix well to avoid lumps, and then pour sauce over meat

Serve with rice or potato salad pg 54

Note: Do not allow water to completely absorb. This dish is served with lots of gravy so add water if necessary.

Serves 4–6 people.

JERK

As I mentioned earlier in this book, food and food preparation greatly defines Jamaican cuisine. Jerk is just one example of how a dish is representative of a people. This recipe is the one recipe that everyone associates with Jamaican food, and boy is it good. The word "Jerk" is a colonial Spanish term, Charqui, meaning preserved or dried meat. Jerk is a method of slow cooking dating back to the Carib-Arawak Indians of Jamaica. It is believed to have been perfected with the Maroons, descendents of slaves who escaped from rule and fled to the Blue Mountains, where they hid for many years. In the mountains, the Maroons practiced and perfected the cooking techniques of their ancestors. However, the Maroons perfected it with the herbs and spices that were introduced to Jamaica by the British, Dutch, French, Spanish, East Indian, West African, Chinese, and Portuguese. The meat would be marinated for hours and then cooked in an outdoor pit lined with pimento wood. Unfortunately, we do not have the access to or the luxury of an outdoor pit, so we use the modern day barbeque (ovens work just fine too). Jerk is cooked slowly, so the meat loses little of its natural juices as well allowing the flavors to intensify.

Jerk recipes have been passed down through generations, but the most common ingredients are allspice, hot chilies, thyme, and salt. There are as many jerk recipes as there are cooks, and as many claims that their recipes are the best. I can honestly say, through much positive feedback, from the many who have tried my jerk recipe, it ranks up there with the best. A bold statement to make, but I'm willing to stand by that claim. Just try it and experience the positive reaction you will get from all those who try it. This is very simple to make, so don't get scared off by the long list of ingredients or cooking and preparations instructions. You can omit the hot pepper from this recipe, but it will change the taste, and to some Jamaicans, once the hot pepper is removed it's no longer "Jerk." The flavors of the jerk seasonings still taste great even without one of the most important ingredients—the hot pepper. So this is for those who can't handle the almighty hot pepper and for kids to enjoy the great flavors of jerk.
You can jerk fish, chicken breasts, ribs, and lamb chops—even a whole leg of lamb. Leave jerk to your imagination. ♥

YOU DON'T HAVE TO GO INTO THE MOUNTAINS ANYMORE TO ENJOY GOOD JERK.

JERK CHICKEN OR JERK PORK

JERK SAUCE

- ½ cup of oil (your choice)
- 1/3 cup of white vinegar
- 4 tablespoons of lime juice
- 3-4 teaspoons of allspice
- 3 teaspoons of salt (or to taste)
- 1 tablespoon of black pepper
- 2 tablespoons of fresh ginger (chopped)
- 1 tablespoon of brown sugar
- 1½ teaspoons of cinnamon
- 2½ tablespoons of fresh thyme (chopped) (or 2 teaspoons of dry)
- 3–4 stalks of small scallions (chopped)
- ½ medium onion (chopped)
- 8 large cloves of garlic (peeled)
- 2–5 scotch bonnet peppers or any hot pepper **(optional) more if you like it really hot**
- ¼ to 1/3 cup of soya sauce (dark, mushroom flavor)
- 1 (4–5-pound) boneless pork shoulder- cut into 2 to 3 pieces for quicker cooking time
- 16 pieces of chicken (legs or thighs)****you can remove the skins to reduce fat intake

I also like to add 1tablespoon each of paprika, cayenne pepper and ground thyme to the sauce.

PREPARATION INSTRUCTIONS FOR JERK SAUCE

STEP 1. To make jerk sauce, put all ingredients in a food processor and blend until a smooth sauce is achieved. Refrigerate if not using immediately. This can last in a jar for several days; up to one week. **Reserve ½ to ¾ cup of sauce: in small pot add the jerk sauce with 1/4 cup of water and cook it for about 40 minutes on low heat.** Use this to brush meat during cooking.

COOKING JERK PORK- This is pictured on pg 81.
Wash pork under cold water and pat dry. Butterfly the meat or cut meat into thirds this will shorten cooking time. (You can ask your butcher to butterfly the pork for you.) In a bowl with the pork, generously rub the marinade all over. Refrigerate for 2 hours, or overnight for best results. Pork is cooked when meat is tender and can easily be pulled with a fork. Only oven **method B** should the pork be cooked until it registers **between 140-155 degrees. See pg 88 for details on resting and carry over cooking. Always make sure to grease your grill to avoid sticking. You can use oil or a cooking spray.**

Grill method A- Preheat grill (barbeque) on low hold a temperature around 200 degrees F and grill with the lid closed for about 2-4 hours or until meat is tender and can easily be pulled with a fork. Brush with reserved sauce and turn several times during the cooking process. (Will be more tender cooked this way).
Grilled method B- Heat one side of the barbeque on high and the other side of the barbeque should not be turned on. (This type of cooking is called indirect cooking). Place a drip pan on the side that has no heat. When the barbeque is hot place the pork on the side of the barbeque that has no heat and cook with the lid closed for 2–5 hours or until meat is tender and can easily be pulled with a fork. Brush with the reserved sauce and turn a few times during the cooking process. (Will be more tender cooked this way).

Oven method A- Preheat oven to 275 degrees. Place the pork on a cookie sheet (on a roasting rack, if possible) and bake uncovered for 2–4 hours; be sure to turn meat over and also brush with reserved sauce several times during cooking. Pork is cooked when it's tender and can be easily pulled with a fork. (Will be more tender cooked this way).

Oven method B- Preheat oven to 350 degrees. Place the pork on a roasting pan (on a roasting rack, if possible) and bake uncovered for 1½ –2 hours; brush with reserved marinade several times during cooking. This method the **Pork is cooked when a meat thermometer, inserted in the thickest part of the roast, registers between 140-155 degrees, or when a fork is inserted and the juices run clear.) *****

Oven method C- Preheat oven to 285-300 degrees. Place pork in roasting pan and cover tightly with foil and bake for 2-5 hours until meat is tender and can easily be pulled with a fork. Remove from pan and place pork onto a cookie sheet that is lined with parchment paper. Brush the sauce that you reserved onto the pork and continue to roast uncovered for 15-20 minutes or until browned on both sides. (Will be more tender cooked this way). Be careful when removing the foil as the steam will be **very hot!!**

COOKING FOR JERK CHICKEN

Remove skins **(optional)** and wash chicken under cold water and pat dry. In a large bowl with the chicken, generously pour the sauce all over, reserving some of the marinade for brushing over the chicken during the cooking process. Refrigerate for 2 hours, or overnight for best results. **Chicken is cooked when pricked with a fork the juices run clear. Always make sure to grease your grill to avoid sticking.**

Grill method A- Preheat grill (barbeque) to low hold a temperature around 200 degrees F and grill with the lid closed for 1½ –2½ hours or until fully cooked; brush with reserved sauce and turn several times during the cooking process. Remove from grill and serve. (Will be more tender cooked this way).

Grill method B- Preheat grill (barbeque) to medium or high and grill with the lid closed for about 25–35 minutes or until fully cooked. Brush with reserved sauce and turn several times during the cooking process.

Grilled method C- Heat one side of the barbeque on high and the other side of the barbeque should not be turned on. (This type of cooking is called indirect cooking). Place a drip pan on the side that has no heat. When the barbeque is hot put the chicken on the side of the barbeque that has no heat and cook with the lid closed for 1½ –4 hours or until done, basting with the reserved sauce several times. (Will be more tender cooked this way).

Oven method A- Preheat oven to 280 degrees. Place the chicken in a roasting pan (on a roasting rack, if possible) in a single layer and bake uncovered for 1½ –2½ hours until done; turn chicken and baste with reserved sauce several times during cooking. (Will be more tender cooked this way).

Oven method B- Preheat oven to 350 degrees. Place the chicken in a roasting pan (on a roasting rack, if possible) in a single layer and bake uncovered for 35–45 minutes until done; turn chicken and baste with reserved sauce several times during cooking. ****** (Chicken is cooked when a fork is inserted and the juices run clear.)******

Truly worth the wait! Get yourself a cold red stripe beer or a cold cooler and enjoy the weather.
Slice or cut meat into pieces. This is traditionally served with hardough bread or festival pg 20.

A great dipping sauce would be the spicy mango sauce on pg 86-87. Serve with mango salsa pg 15. If you can find pimento wood create smoke pouches as directed on pgs 85- 86 barbeque ribs and indirect grilling.

SEAFOOD AND FISH

I love seafood and fish, so this is definitely one of my favorite sections of the book. Jamaica's national dish is Ackee and Salt Fish, which I happen to love and I hope you will give it a try. If you are not that adventurous, then try my Grilled Salmon or Broiled Salmon; they are both very tasty and easy to put together. If you like it hot, then Peppered Shrimp is the dish for you, and for those of you who are in a rush, the Stir Fried Shrimp is just what you are looking for. All the dishes in this section are very easy to prepare, so you will have plenty of time to enjoy a drink and relax with family and friends or that special someone.

PICTURE YOURSELF TAKING A NICE LONG WALK WITH THE HEAT OF THE SUN MELTING ALL YOUR PROBLEMS AWAY.

ACKEE AND SALT FISH

This is Jamaica's national dish. This is traditionally served for breakfast, but is great anytime of the day. I love this. Lord have mercy! This is pictured on pg 82.♥

- ➢ 3 cups of salt fish (cooked, bones removed, and then shredded)
- ➢ 1 can of ackee (**Grace products**, sold in most grocery stores or in west Indian stores)
- ➢ 2 stalks of scallions (chopped)
- ➢ 1 clove of garlic minced
- ➢ 1 medium onion (sliced)
- ➢ 2 cups of tomatoes (chopped)
- ➢ 1 whole scotch bonnet pepper **(optional)**
- ➢ 1/3 cup of oil (vegetable)
- ➢ 1 teaspoon of ground thyme
- ➢ salt and lots of black pepper

COOKING AND PREPARATION INSTRUCTIONS

STEP 1.   Turn the heat to medium. Place fry pan on heat and add oil. Add the scallions, onion, garlic, and scotch bonnet to the hot oil and cook for 5 minutes.

STEP 2.   Add tomatoes and black pepper and cook for 2 more minutes.

STEP 3.   Add the salt fish, thyme and cook for 2 more minutes.

STEP 4.   Drain the ackee and add to pan; cook for 5 minutes more, until heated thoroughly. Taste for salt. You can substitute the 1 can of ackee with 1 can of calalloo.

This is traditionally served with boiled green banana and boiled or fried dumplings pg 22.

Note: Salt fish is very salty, so to remove the excess salt, you can either boil several times, changing the water after each boil, or you can soak overnight and then boil the salt fish for 15 minutes, or until cooked. Whichever method you choose, once the fish is cooked, shred (flake), so you have it ready to add to any dish.

They also eat this with roasted breadfruit, or steamed calalloo pg 60 which is grown in Jamaica and you can purchase in West Indian stores, fresh or in cans. You can serve with plantain pg 65, sweet potatoes, and other root vegetables. Use your imagination.

This is easy to double.

SUBSTITUTE SALT FISH with sole, bluefish, or white fish, and even crabmeat.

Serves 4 people.

SALT FISH CASSEROLE

How many ways can you enjoy salt fish? Well, as you can see, the Jamaicans have found quite a few tasty dishes using the well loved salt fish. ♥

- 3 cups of salt fish (cooked, bones removed, and flaked/shredded)
- 6 medium to large potatoes (boiled, sliced, and salted to taste)
- 6 large eggs (boiled and sliced)
- ¼ cup of oil (your choice)
- 1 medium onion (finely chopped)
- 4 cloves of garlic (minced)
- 1 green pepper (finely chopped)
- 2 tablespoons of fresh thyme (finely chopped)
- 1 teaspoon of paprika and allspice
- 3 stalks of scallions (finely chopped)
- scotch bonnet pepper or any hot pepper (finely chopped) **(optional)**
- 1 tomato (chopped)
- ½ cup of heavy cream
- 3-4 tablespoons of white (All purpose) flour
- salt and black pepper to taste
- ¼ cup of breadcrumbs
- mint or cilantro

COOKING AND PREPARATION INSTRUCTIONS

STEP 1.   Turn the heat to medium. Place fry pan on heat and add ¼ cup of the oil. Add the onion, garlic, green pepper, thyme, paprika, scallions, and hot pepper into the hot oil and sauté for 5 minutes. Add tomatoes, salt fish, and cook for 2 minutes more. Remove from heat, add cream and flour and mix well. Taste for salt and black pepper.

STEP 2.   Generously grease the bottom of a casserole pan or medium lasagna pan.

STEP 3.   In layers, arrange the sliced potatoes, eggs, and salt fish mixture; continue to layer until finished. Top with breadcrumbs; drizzle top with oil and mint or cilantro.

STEP 4.   In a 350 degree oven, bake covered for about 45 minutes and then 5–10 minutes uncovered, until breadcrumbs become golden. Let rest for 15 minutes before serving.

Note: Salt fish is very salty, so to remove the excess salt, you can either boil several times, changing the water after each boil, or you can soak overnight and then boil the salt fish for 15 minutes or until cooked. Whichever method you choose, once the fish is cooked, shred (flake), so you have it ready to add to any dish.

SUBSTITUTE SALT FISH with sole, any white fish, or shredded crab

Serve with rice or a fresh salad.

Serves 4–6 people.

PICK UP SALT FISH

This is very good. I love it with fried dumplings. I remember the first time I had it for breakfast at my in-laws' house. I kept thinking to myself, what smells so good? This is pictured on pg 81. ❤

- ➢ 3½ cups of salt fish (cooked, bones removed, and flaked/shredded)
- ➢ 2 stalks of scallions (chopped)
- ➢ 1 medium onion (sliced)
- ➢ ½ of a green pepper chopped **(optional)**
- ➢ 2 cloves garlic (finely minced)
- ➢ 1 scotch bonnet pepper or any hot pepper (finely chopped) **(optional)**
- ➢ 2 medium tomatoes (chopped)
- ➢ 1/3 cup of oil (vegetable)
- ➢ 2 teaspoons of black pepper or to taste
- ➢ salt to taste

COOKING AND PREPARATION INSTRUCTIONS

STEP 1. Turn the heat to medium. Place fry pan on heat and add the oil. Add the scallions, onion, green pepper, garlic and scotch bonnet to the hot oil and cook for 2–3 minutes.

STEP 2. Add tomatoes and continue to cook on medium for 2 more minutes.

STEP 3. Add the salt fish and black pepper and cook for 10 minutes more. Remove from heat and serve. Taste for salt.

Note: Salt fish is very salty, so to remove the excess salt, you can either boil several times, changing the water after each boil, or you can soak overnight and then boil the salt fish for 15 minutes or until cooked. Whichever method you choose, once the fish is cooked, shred (flake), so you have it ready to add to any dish.

Serve with fried or boiled dumplings, fried plantain, or any boiled root vegetable, such as yams, Jamaican sweet potatoes, or regular sweet potatoes, steamed callaloo pg 60 . Served traditionally for breakfast, but you can enjoy this anytime. For more of a meal you can serve with rice and a fresh salad.

SUBSTITUTE SALT FISH with sole, any white fish, or shredded crab.

Easy to double.

Serves 3–4 people.

RUNDOWN

This is an unusual name, and I cannot begin to tell you where its name originated; however, what I can tell you is that it is very good. This is an easier version of Rundown; my recipe uses canned coconut milk. ♥

- ➢ 2 pounds of pickled mackerel (cut into pieces)
- ➢ 1½ cups of canned coconut milk (**Grace product** or your choice)
- ➢ ½ cup of water
- ➢ 1 onion (chopped)
- ➢ 3 stalks of scallions (chopped)
- ➢ 3 cloves of garlic (finely chopped)
- ➢ 1 tablespoon of fresh thyme (finely chopped)
- ➢ 1 scotch bonnet pepper or any hot pepper (finely chopped) **optional**
- ➢ 1 medium tomato (chopped)
- ➢ salt and black pepper to taste

COOKING AND PREPARATION INSTRUCTIONS

STEP 1. Soak the pickled mackerel for a couple of hours or overnight in fridge, to help remove the salt. Clean well and cut into pieces about 2-inch thick.

STEP 2. In a fry pan on medium heat cook coconut milk, water, onion, scallions, garlic, thyme, black pepper and scotch bonnet until it resembles curdled custard or looks oily, this should take about 25 minutes

STEP 3. Add fish and tomato; cook for 15–20 minutes more, taste for seasonings. Remove from heat and pour over food, 2 dumplings per person.

Serve with food.

FOOD: Boiled green banana, boiled plantain pg 65, Jamaican sweet potatoes, yams, regular sweet potatoes, regular potatoes, and boiled dumplings pg 22; your choice.

SUBSTITUTE PICKLED MACKEREL with salt fish (salt cod), herring, shad, or salmon.

Note: This should not be creamy, but you don't want it to be too watery either.

Serves 3–4 people.

HOLY MACKEREL WITH ONION AND PEPPER

This is another quick and easy meal. It resembles sardines, but in my opinion, tastes better. ♥

- ➢ 2 cans of jack mackerel in sauce (**Grace products**)
- ➢ 3 tablespoons of oil (your choice)
- ➢ 3 stalks of scallions (chopped)
- ➢ 1 medium onion (sliced)
- ➢ 1 green pepper (chopped into small cubes)
- ➢ 1 tablespoon of fresh thyme (finely chopped)
- ➢ 1 whole scotch bonnet pepper or any hot pepper (finely chopped) **(optional)**
- ➢ ¼–1/3 cup of coconut milk **(optional)** (**Grace product** or your choice)
- ➢ 1¼ cups of water
- ➢ salt and black pepper to taste

COOKING AND PREPARATION INSTRUCTIONS

STEP 1.   Turn the heat to medium. Place fry pan on heat and add the oil. Add the scallions, onion, and green pepper to the hot oil and sauté for 2 minutes.

STEP 2.   Add jack mackerel with sauce, along with thyme, salt, black pepper, scotch bonnet, coconut milk, and water. Cook for about 15–20 minutes, until the liquid has reduced to half and formed a sauce; check for salt and adjust seasonings to taste.

This is traditionally served with boiled dumplings, boiled green bananas, boiled plantain pg 65, sweet potatoes, or yams. You can also serve with rice and a fresh salad.

Serves 3–4 people.

STIR FRIED SHRIMP

Not so traditional, but with all the ingredients indigenous to Jamaica, it makes this shrimp dish one worth making. This is pictured on pg 81. ❤

- 3 pounds of medium shrimp (cleaned and shells removed)
- 1–2 tablespoons of oil (your choice)
- 3 stalks of scallions (chopped)
- 4 cloves of garlic (finely chopped)
- 1 tablespoon of fresh ginger (finely chopped)
- ½ of an onion (chopped)
- 1 scotch bonnet pepper or any hot pepper (finely chopped) **(optional)**
- 1 green pepper (chopped into cubes)
- 1 red pepper (chopped into cubes)
- ½ teaspoon of allspice
- 2½ tablespoons of hoisin sauce
- 2 tablespoons of sesame oil
- 1 tablespoon of soya sauce
- ¾ cups of water or chicken broth
- 2 tablespoons of corn starch
- salt and black pepper to taste

COOKING AND PREPARATION INSTRUCTIONS

STEP 1. Turn the heat to medium. Place fry pan or wok on heat and add oil. Add the scallions, garlic, ginger, onion, and hot pepper to the hot oil and cook for 2–3 minutes.

STEP 2. Add green pepper, red pepper, and allspice, and give a good stir. Add hoisin sauce, sesame oil, and soya sauce, and continue to fry on medium heat for 5–10 minutes, mixing often (depending on how soft you like your peppers).

STEP 3. In a bowl with ¾ cup water or chicken broth, add cornstarch; mix well.

STEP 4. In the fry pan add shrimp, salt and black pepper, and cornstarch mixture, and cook until shrimp are done. You will have thick sauce to pour over rice. (Shrimps are cooked when they turn pink/opaque and curl up slightly.) Serve with rice.

SUBSTITUTE SHRIMP with cubed pork or cubed chicken breasts.

Serves 3–4 people.

CURRY SHRIMP

This is too good to pass up. This is very easy to prepare and even quicker to disappear. This is really nice for a dinner party. ❤

- ➢ 3 pounds of shrimp (cleaned and shells removed)
- ➢ 1 green pepper (chopped into cubes) **(optional)**
- ➢ 3 tablespoons of oil (your choice)
- ➢ 4 cloves of garlic (finely chopped)
- ➢ 2 stalks of scallions (chopped)
- ➢ ½ medium onion (finely chopped)
- ➢ 1 tablespoon of fresh ginger (finely chopped)
- ➢ 1 scotch bonnet pepper or any hot pepper (finely chopped)
- ➢ 2–3 tablespoons of curry powder (preferably a Jamaican—**Grace products**—or Caribbean curry
- ➢ 2 tablespoons of cornstarch + (more if necessary)
- ➢ 1½ cups of water + (more water if necessary)
- ➢ 1 tablespoon of fresh thyme (finely chopped)
- ➢ 2 cups of chopped cubed tomatoes (optional)
- ➢ salt and black pepper to taste

COOKING AND PREPARATION INSTRUCTIONS

STEP 1. Turn the heat to medium. Place fry pan on heat and add the oil. Add the garlic, scallions, onion, ginger, curry powder, and hot pepper to the hot oil and cook for 2–3 minutes.

STEP 2. In a bowl add the water and cornstarch and stir until smooth. Add the cornstarch mixture along with the thyme, salt, and black pepper to the pan and cook on medium heat for 10 minutes, stirring occasionally. Sauce should have thickened.

STEP 3. And chopped tomatoes **(optional) cook for 2 minutes then** add the shrimp and cook until shrimps are done; turns a pink/opaque color. Check for seasonings, and adjust to taste. You should end up with a sauce (gravy) enough to pour over the rice. If necessary add more water.

Tip: If the liquid is still too watery, add 2-3 tablespoons of cornstarch and mix it with enough water until it has the consistency of heavy cream (smooth). While on medium heat, remove meat from pot. Add flour mixture to the pot slowly until it thickens. Mix well to avoid lumps, and then pour sauce over meat

SUBSTITUTE SHRIMP with sliced chicken breasts; increase-cooking time.

Serve over rice and with a fresh salad.

Your friends will be impressed if you serve this.

Serves 4 people.

HERE ARE MY GORGEOUS NIECES GETTING READY TO GO OUT TO
DINNER.

SEEN HERE ARE AUNTIE SANNIE, MY HUSBAND STEVE AND PHILLIS
ENJOYING A STROLL IN KINGSTON FOR SOME ICE CREAM.

PEPPERED SHRIMP

This dish can be found being sold along the roadside in Jamaica. I really loved them, so here is my version. This is served as a snack. So, from the roadside of Jamaica to my kitchen, and now to yours … This is so good; trust me, you can't just have a few, so make sure to have an empty stomach so that you can fill up. ❤

- ➢ 3 pounds of shrimp (wash and pat dry very well; do not remove shell)
- ➢ 1/3 to ½ cup of oil (your choice) you can get away with ¼ cup
- ➢ 5 cloves of garlic (finely chopped)
- ➢ 1½ tablespoons of fresh ginger (finely chopped)
- ➢ 3–4 scotch bonnet peppers or any hot pepper of choice (chopped) **(optional)**
- ➢ 1–1½ teaspoons of salt or to taste
- ➢ 3 teaspoons of paprika
- ➢ black pepper to taste
- ➢ 3 tablespoons of vinegar
- ➢ 1 tablespoon of fresh lime juice

COOKING AND PREPARATION INSTRUCTIONS

STEP 1.   Turn the heat to medium. Place fry pan on heat and add the oil. Add the garlic, ginger, and scotch bonnet to the hot oil and sauté for a few minutes.

STEP 2.   To the pan add the shrimp and salt, paprika, and black pepper; stir well.

STEP 3.   Add vinegar and lime and continue to cook on medium heat for 6–7 minutes. When shrimp are done they turn pink and curl slightly. Remove from heat.

Serve warm or cold.

Serves 3–4 people as an appetizer.

PEPPERED SHRIMP FOUND ALONG THE ROADSIDE—ONLY IN JAMAICA.

HERE ARE HOWIE AND JODY ENJOYING THE DAY AND THINKING OF
DRIVING AROUND THE ISLAND LOOKING FOR THOSE FAMOUS SHRIMP
FOUND ONLY BY THE ROADSIDE.

COCONUT CURRY SHRIMP

"Let's get together and feel all right." This is too good to pass up. This is easy to prepare and even quicker to disappear. This is really nice for a dinner party. This is pictured on pg 82. ♥

- ➢ 3 pounds of shrimp (washed peeled and de-veined)
- ➢ ¼ cup of oil (your choice)
- ➢ 4 cloves of garlic (finely chopped)
- ➢ 3 stalks of scallions (chopped)
- ➢ ½ medium onion (finely chopped)
- ➢ 1 tablespoon of fresh ginger (finely chopped)
- ➢ 1 scotch bonnet pepper or any hot pepper (chopped) **(optional)**
- ➢ 2 tablespoons of curry powder (preferably a Jamaican—**Grace products**—or Caribbean curry)
- ➢ 2 tablespoons of cornstarch + (more if necessary)
- ➢ ½ cup of coconut milk **(Grace products** or your choice)
- ➢ 1½ cups of water + (more water if necessary)
- ➢ 2 tablespoons of fresh thyme (finely chopped)
- ➢ 2 cups of chopped cubed tomatoes (optional)
- ➢ salt and black pepper to taste

COOKING AND PREPARATION INSTRUCTIONS

STEP 1. Turn the heat to medium. Place fry pan on heat and add oil. Add the garlic, scallions, onion, ginger, curry powder, and hot pepper to the hot oil and cook for about 2–3 minutes.

STEP 2. In a bowl add the water and cornstarch and stir until smooth then add mixture with the coconut milk, thyme, salt, and black pepper to the pan and cook on low heat for 10 -12 minutes, stirring occasionally. Sauce should have reduced and thickened.

STEP 3. And chopped tomatoes **(optional) cook for 2 minutes then** add the shrimp and cook until done; turns a pink/opaque color. Check for seasonings, and adjust to taste. You should end up with a sauce (gravy) to pour over the rice. If necessary add more water.

Tip: If the liquid is still too watery, add 2-3 tablespoons of cornstarch and mix it with enough water until it has the consistency of heavy cream (smooth). While on medium heat, remove meat from pot. Add flour mixture to the pot slowly until it thickens. Mix well to avoid lumps, and then pour sauce over meat

SUBSTITUTE SHRIMP with sliced chicken breasts; increase cooking time.

Serve over rice and with a fresh salad.

Your friends will be impressed if you serve this.

Serves 4 people.

SEASONED FISH WITH ONION AND TOMATO

This is a nice way to enjoy whole fish, and it's easy to make and really tasty. ♥

- 1 (3½-pound) fish (red snapper)
- salt and black pepper to taste
- ¼ cup of white (All purpose) flour
- 4 cloves of garlic (finely chopped)
- 1 tablespoon of fresh ginger (finely chopped)
- 3 stalks of scallions (finely chopped)
- 1 large onion (sliced)
- 2 tomatoes (chopped)
- 2 tablespoons of fresh thyme (finely chopped)
- 1 teaspoon of allspice and of paprika
- 1 scotch bonnet pepper or any hot pepper (finely chopped) **(optional)**
- 1 tablespoon of vinegar
- 1 cup of water
- 1/3 cup of oil (your choice)
- ¼ cup of corn meal
- cornstarch

COOKING AND PREPARATION INSTRUCTIONS

STEP 1. Wash fish with cold water, pat dry. Season fish with salt and black pepper and then coat both sides of the fish with cornmeal. Set aside.

STEP 2. Turn the heat to medium. Place fry pan or wok on heat and add oil. Add the fish to the hot oil and fry until both sides are golden brown. Remove and set aside. Add the sliced onion and sauté for about 3–4 minutes, or until soft; remove and place in a dish. Set aside.

STEP 3. In the same pan add more oil if necessary and on medium heat sauté the garlic, ginger and scallions for a few minutes. Add tomatoes, thyme, allspice, paprika, hot pepper, salt, and black pepper; cook for an additional minute more and then add the water and vinegar; cook for 5 minutes. Taste for seasonings.

STEP 4. Add fish and the fried onion from Step 2; continue cook on medium heat for 10-15 minutes until fish is fully cooked. Fish is cooked when touched with a fork it flakes easily.

Tip: If the liquid is still too watery, add 2-3 tablespoons of cornstarch and mix it with enough water until it has the consistency of heavy cream (smooth). While on medium heat, remove meat from pot. Add flour mixture to the pot slowly until it thickens. Mix well to avoid lumps, and then pour sauce over meat

Serve with rice and salad.

Serves 3 people.

GRILLED RED SNAPPER

This will become a favorite grilled fish recipe, because it's so easy to put together and the ingredients work together so well. ♥

- 1 fish (3–3½-pound) red snapper or fish of choice
- 5 cloves of garlic (finely chopped)
- 3 stalks of scallions (chopped)
- 2 teaspoons of fresh ginger (finely chopped)
- 2 tablespoons of fresh thyme (finely chopped)
- 2 tomatoes (sliced and season with salt)
- 1 large onion (sliced)
- 1 green pepper (sliced)
- 1 scotch bonnet pepper or any hot pepper (chopped) **(optional)**
- 1/3 cup of oil (your choice)
- 2 tablespoons of fresh lime juice + **1 lime sliced**
- salt and black pepper

COOKING AND PREPARATION INSTRUCTIONS

STEP 1. Turn the heat to medium. Place fry pan or wok on heat and add oil. Add garlic, scallions, ginger, and hot pepper to hot oil and sauté until soft. Add thyme, and cook for 1 minute more. Set aside to cool.

STEP 2. Place fish in foil and season fish with salt and pepper; pour half of the cooled oil mixture from Step 1 on top of the fish and the other half of the oil mixture in the cavity of the fish.

STEP 3. Add sliced tomatoes, onion, pepper, and slices of lime also in the cavity of the fish. Wrap the fish very well in foil paper.

STEP 4. Preheat barbeque to medium and make sure to grease the grill to avoid sticking.

STEP 5. Place the wrapped fish directly on the grill or you can place the foil wrap in a BBQ grill basket and grill for 12-15 minutes, turning once. Remove from foil and squeeze lime and drizzle with more oil. Fish is cooked when touched with fork it flakes easily.

Serve with just about anything, and go ahead and have yourself a cool drink.

Note: You can bake in a 350 degree oven on a cookie sheet or baking pan wrapped with foil for about 25–30 minutes or until cooked. You can also place the fish directly on a greased cookie sheet or baking pan, turning one time halfway into cooking, cook for about 25 minutes.

This is great with mango salsa pg 15, tomato and pepper relish pg 14or mango and papaya chutney pg 17.

Serves 2-3 people.

BREADED FISH FILLETS WITH SPICY MAYO SAUCE

Feeling good right about now, this tastes so good and is also healthy for you, because the fish is baked and not fried. This will serve 3 to 4 people with a side dish. ♥

- ➢ 3½ pounds of fish fillets (red snapper, ocean perch, or your favorite)
- ➢ salt and black pepper to taste
- ➢ 1/3 cup of corn meal
- ➢ ¾ cup of unflavored breadcrumbs
- ➢ 2 teaspoons each of allspice and **ground garlic powder**
- ➢ 1 tablespoon of fresh thyme (finely chopped) or 1 teaspoon of ground thyme
- ➢ 2 teaspoon of paprika
- ➢ 2 egg
- ➢ ¼ cup water
- ➢ ¼–1/3 oil (your choice)
- ➢ mint or coriander
- ➢ **SPICY MAYO SAUCE**
- ➢ 1 cup of light mayonnaise
- ➢ 1/3 cup of sour cream
- ➢ 2 tablespoons of crushed red pepper sauce (**Grace products** or your choice)
- ➢ 1 tablespoon of scallions (finely chopped)
- ➢ 1 tablespoon of oil (your choice)
- ➢ 1 tablespoon of fresh lime juice
- ➢ salt and black pepper to taste

COOKING AND PREPARATION INSTRUCTIONS

STEP 1. **For spicy mayo sauce-** In a bowl combine all ingredients together; mix very well. Taste for seasonings. Refrigerate until ready to use.

STEP 2. Wash fish under cold water very well and pat dry, and then add salt and black pepper. In a bowl add the corn meal and some more salt for taste. In a separate bowl with the breadcrumbs, add the allspice, garlic powder, thyme, paprika, and more salt; mix well. In another bowl add the eggs with ¼ cup water, and beat well.

STEP 3. Dust fish with corn meal; dip into the egg mixture and then generously coat the fish with the breadcrumb mixture. Place the fillets on a plate, cover, and refrigerate until ready to cook.

STEP 4. Preheat oven to 350 degrees. Place fish fillets in a single layer on a cookie sheet or baking pan lined with parchment paper. Grease parchment paper with oil generously and drizzle more oil on top of the fish.

STEP 5. Bake for 10–18 minutes (depending on the size of your fillet), turning fish over halfway into cooking. When fish is done it will flake easily. For a crispier fish, broil for 2 minutes at the very end.

STEP 6. Transfer to individual plates and top with spicy mayo sauce and with mint, or serve with lime wedges only.

Serve with coleslaw pg 53, potato salad pg 54, or seasonal vegetables. Other great sauces or topping would be tomato and pepper relish pg 14, fresh garlic and thyme sauce pg 17 , or spicy mango sauce pg 93.

BROWN STEW FISH

Although the list of ingredients may seem very long, this can be put together rather quickly, and believe me, it's worth the extra work. ♥

- ➤ 4 red snapper steaks or your favorite fish
- ➤ salt and black pepper to taste
- ➤ 1/3 cup of flour
- ➤ 4 cloves of garlic (finely chopped)
- ➤ 3 stalks of scallions (chopped)
- ➤ 1 medium onion (sliced)
- ➤ 1 green pepper (chopped into cubes)
- ➤ 2 teaspoons of paprika
- ➤ 1½ tablespoons of allspice
- ➤ 2 tomatoes (chopped)
- ➤ 2 tablespoons of fresh thyme (finely chopped)
- ➤ 2 teaspoons of fresh ginger (finely chopped)
- ➤ 1 scotch bonnet pepper or any hot pepper(finely chopped) **(optional)**
- ➤ 2 tablespoons of soya sauce
- ➤ 1 cup of water + (more water if necessary)
- ➤ 1 tablespoon of fresh lime juice
- ➤ ¼ cup of oil (your choice)
- ➤ cornstarch (if necessary)

COOKING AND PREPARATION INSTRUCTIONS

STEP 1. Clean fish with cold water and pat dry; add salt and black pepper. Flour both sides well and set aside.

STEP 2. Turn the heat to medium. Place fry pan or wok on heat and add oil. Add the fish to the hot oil and brown about 5 minutes per side. Remove fish and set aside.

STEP 3. Return fry pan or wok to the stovetop on medium heat. Cook the garlic, scallions, onion, green pepper, paprika, allspice, tomatoes, thyme, ginger, hot pepper, and soya sauce for a few minutes and then add water, lime juice, and some more salt.

STEP 4. Raise the heat to high and bring to a boil and cook for additional 10 minutes.

STEP 5. Reduce heat to medium or low and return the fish to the fry pan or wok. Cook until thickened and fish is done; about 15 minutes. The fish will flake easily when done.

Tip: If the liquid is still too watery, add 2-3 tablespoons of cornstarch and mix it with enough water until it has the consistency of heavy cream (smooth). While on medium heat, remove meat from pot. Add flour mixture to the pot slowly until it thickens. Mix well to avoid lumps, and then pour sauce over meat

Serve with any rice dish, potato salad pg 54, or seasonal vegetables.

Serves 4 people.

BROWN STEW FISH

ALWAYS READY FOR A GOOD TIME—LOTS OF FUN AND LAUGHTER BETWEEN FAMILY AND FRIENDS.

SALMON IN CURRY AND COCONUT SAUCE

This is so good, but if you don't like coconut, just omit and cook with curry only (it is also very good this way). This would be good with Red Snapper steaks too. This is pictured on page 84. ♥

- ➢ 4 salmon steaks
- ➢ 3 tablespoons of oil (your choice)
- ➢ 4 cloves of garlic (finely chopped)
- ➢ 3 stalks of scallions (finely chopped)
- ➢ 1 teaspoon of fresh ginger (finely chopped)
- ➢ 1 medium onion (finely chopped)
- ➢ 1 scotch bonnet pepper or any hot pepper (chopped) **(optional)**
- ➢ 2-3 tablespoons of curry powder (preferably a Jamaican—**Grace products**—or Caribbean curry
- ➢ 1-2 tablespoons of fresh thyme (finely chopped)
- ➢ ½ cup of coconut milk (Grace products or your choice)
- ➢ salt and black pepper to taste
- ➢ 2 cups of water + ¼ cup
- ➢ 2 cups of roughly chopped tomatoes **(optional)**
- ➢ cornstarch (if necessary)

COOKING AND PREPARATION INSTRUCTIONS

STEP 1. Wash the salmon steaks very well; add salt and black pepper. Set aside.

STEP 2. Turn the heat to medium. Place fry pan or wok on heat and add the oil. Add the garlic, scallions, ginger, onion, curry powder, and hot pepper to the hot oil and cook for 2–3 minutes.

STEP 3. Add coconut milk, thyme, salt, black pepper, and 2 **cups of water**. Cook on medium heat for 10-15 minutes or until liquid has reduced and thickened.

STEP 4. And chopped tomatoes **(optional) cook for 2 minutes then** add salmon and cook for 12-15 more minutes or until cooked; taste for salt and pepper. The fish will flake easily when done. If sauce is too thick add water.

Tip: If the liquid is still too watery, add 2-3 tablespoons of cornstarch and mix it with enough water until it has the consistency of heavy cream (smooth). While on medium heat, remove meat from pot. Add flour mixture to the pot slowly until it thickens. Mix well to avoid lumps, and then pour sauce over meat

Serve with rice and plantain pg 65 or any of your favorite side dishes.

SUBSTITUTE SALMON with red snapper, about 2 inches thick.

Serves 4 people.

GRILLED SALMON

So good, and healthy for you too! The ingredients work so well with salmon. This is always a big hit and requested by my family all the time. ♥

- 4 salmon steaks
- 3 stalks of scallions (chopped)
- 3 cloves of garlic (chopped)
- 1 scotch bonnet pepper or any hot pepper (chopped) **(optional)**
- 1 tablespoon of fresh ginger (chopped)
- 2 tablespoons of fresh thyme chopped finely
- 2 tablespoons each of finely chopped mint or cilantro
- 2 tablespoons of soya sauce (dark, mushroom flavor)
- 1 teaspoon of allspice
- salt and black pepper
- $\frac{1}{4}$ cup of oil (your choice)
- 2 tablespoons of fresh lime juice

COOKING AND PREPARATION INSTRUCTIONS

STEP 1.   In a large bowl add the scallions, garlic, hot pepper, ginger, thyme, mint or coriander, soya sauce, allspice, salt, black pepper, and oil, and mix well. Add salmon to the mixture and mix; refrigerate for 1–2 hours.

STEP 2.   Preheat barbeque to medium and make sure to grease the grill to avoid sticking.

STEP 3.   Remove fish from fridge and add the lime juice. Grill the salmon for about 5 minutes per side or until cooked.

STEP 4.   Remove salmon from grill; drizzle additional lime and fresh cilantro and mint. The fish will flake easily when done.

Serve with salad and rice. This would be great served with any of the condiments detailed in my book, such as papaya mint salsa pg 14, mango salsa pg 15, avocado and tomato salsa pg 15, mango and papaya chutney pg 17 or fresh garlic and thyme sauce pg 17.

Serves 4 people

BROILED SALMON

This is really good and really tender. Try it, and you will love it as much as I do. ♥

- ➤ 4 salmon fillets (2 inches thick)
- ➤ salt and black pepper
- ➤ ½ teaspoon of allspice
- ➤ 3 cloves of garlic (finely chopped)
- ➤ 2 stalks of scallions (finely chopped)
- ➤ 1 tablespoon of fresh ginger (finely chopped)
- ➤ 1 tablespoon of fresh thyme (finely chopped)
- ➤ 1/3 cup of hoisin sauce
- ➤ 2 tablespoons of sesame oil
- ➤ 1 tablespoon of soya sauce
- ➤ 1 tablespoon of chili garlic sauce or crushed red pepper sauce **(optional)**
- ➤ 1 tablespoon of fresh limejuice

COOKING AND PREPARATION INSTRUCTIONS

STEP 1. Wash salmon fillets and pat dry; add salt and black pepper.

STEP 2. In a large bowl whisk together allspice, garlic, scallions, ginger, thyme, hoisin sauce, sesame oil, soya sauce, and chili garlic sauce. Add salmon to marinade and turn occasionally. Cover and refrigerate for 2–3 hours.

STEP 3. Place salmon on a parchment/greased baking sheet and broil for 5 minutes per side or until cooked. The fish will flake easily when done.

SUBSTITUTE SALMON with red snapper steaks or even pork steaks (increase cooking time for pork steaks).

Serve with rice and peas pg 48, potato salad pg 55, seasonal vegetables, and many more.

Serves 4 people.

BROILED SALMON

ENJOYING A SUNSET CRUISE WITH A FEW DRINKS AND GOOD FRIENDS—DOES IT GET ANY BETTER THAN THIS?

CURRIED KING CRAB LEGS

My favorite seafood is king crab legs, so it's fitting that I add another of my favorite things, which is curry, and the combination is outstanding. This is a little messy, but well worth it. Just make sure to have plenty of napkins on hand. ❤

- 3–3 ½ pounds of king crab legs (in shells, wash and make sure you slit each piece)
- 3 stalks of scallions (finely chopped)
- 4 cloves of garlic (finely chopped)
- 1 tablespoon of fresh thyme (finely chopped)
- 1 small onion (finely chopped)
- 1 tablespoon of fresh ginger (finely chopped)
- 2–3 tablespoons of curry powder (preferably a Jamaican—**Grace products**—or Caribbean curry)
- 2 tablespoons of cornstarch + (more cornstarch if necessary)
- 2 cups of water + (more water if necessary)
- salt and black pepper
- 1 tablespoon of butter
- 3 tablespoons of oil (your choice)

COOKING AND PREPARATION INSTRUCTIONS

STEP 1. Turn the heat to medium. Place fry pan or wok on heat and add the oil. Add the scallions, garlic, thyme, onion, and ginger to the hot oil and cook for 2–3 minutes.

STEP 2. Add the crab and stir in curry; mix well for about 2 minutes and then add water; cook covered for 20 minutes. Mix often to avoid sticking and drying out.

STEP 3. Add butter and cook uncovered for 5-7 more minutes or until mixture has reduced and liquid thickens. Do not allow liquid in pot to completely absorb, if necessary add water.

Tip: If the liquid is still too watery, add 2-3 tablespoons of cornstarch and mix it with enough water until it has the consistency of heavy cream (smooth). While on medium heat, remove meat from pot. Add flour mixture to the pot slowly until it thickens. Mix well to avoid lumps, and then pour sauce over meat

Variation: Curried crab and/or lobster meat, 3½ pounds (cooked). This would suit a fancier dinner party.
- Same ingredients as above for curried king crab leg, however, use only 1½ cups of water.

COOKING AND PREPARATION INSTRUCTIONS

STEP 1. Turn the heat to medium. Place fry pan or wok on heat and add the oil. Add the scallions, garlic, thyme, onion, and ginger to the hot oil and cook for 2–3 minutes.

STEP 2. Add curry and stir well for about 1 minute, add water and stir the cornstarch with a whisk to avoid any lumps. Cook on medium heat for 10-12 minutes, until mixture has reduced.

STEP 3. Add crab or lobster meat and butter and cook for 5 more minutes. Do not allow liquid in pot to completely absorb, if necessary add more water.

STEP 4. If liquid in pan is too watery see tip from above

Serve with salad or rice.
Serves 4 people.

CURRIED CRAB

MY NIECE, ELISABETH, ALWAYS HAPPY ENJOYING TIME IN THE
WATER.

DESSERTS AND DRINKS

I could not write a cookbook without including a section on sweets. Jamaicans definitely have a sweet tooth, and from personal experience, a good eye for candy as well. A prime retirement spot for dentists, the Island is a mixture of British and local influences. The British left their mark with desserts such as the Sweet Potato and Bread Pudding that Jamaicans love to prepare to this very day. The Island provides sweet sugar cane, which is turned into rum, another favorite pastime of the diehard locals. The recipes in my book are a combination of the old and the new. Be adventurous with the Easter Bun recipe, or play it safe with the Banana Bread, but whichever you choose, just don't blame me for the cavities. It's all up to you; after all, cooking has always been about choices, and that's what I'm offering. Take a chance and experience what Jamaicans have been for many years. Enjoy your sweets with one of the best coffees—Blue Mountain—grown in the mountains of Jamaica. If sweets aren't your cup of tea, try one or more of their exotic drinks; after a few, you just might like any dessert in this book. Have fun and enjoy the laughter and stories that will be associated with any dessert or drink. My favorite rum is the Appleton Jamaica Rum; however, you can use any kind you like. Note, anytime I mention milk in my recipes you can use, whole milk, low fat, skim, 1% and 2 % however the fatter the milk the better the end result

FEELIN' FINE, ALWAYS IN JAMAICA.

BANANA FRITTERS

This is a quick and easy dessert to prepare for all your friends and family to enjoy. The aroma will quickly engulf your kitchen and will draw people to come see what that incredible smell is. ❤

- 3 large bananas
- 1 large egg (beaten)
- 4 tablespoons of granulated sugar
- 3 teaspoons of baking powder
- ½ cup of milk (2%)
- 1 cup of white (All purpose) flour
- 1 tablespoon of cinnamon
- 1 teaspoon of grated nutmeg
- vegetable oil for frying

COOKING AND PREPARATION INSTRUCTIONS

STEP 1.　Mash bananas until creamed, and set aside.

STEP 2.　Combine flour, baking powder, sugar, cinnamon, and nutmeg.

STEP 3.　Add milk, beaten egg and bananas to flour mixture and combine well. If you find the mixture too thick add more milk, and if too thin add more flour. Batter should have consistency to be dropped easily in hot oil.

STEP 4.　In hot oil, spoon in a scoop (about 1 tablespoon) of the batter into the frying pan and fry on medium heat until golden and crisp on both sides, about 5 minutes per side

STEP 5.　Drain on paper towels and serve warm. Sprinkle powdered sugar on top **(optional)**.

Serve with whipped cream for a fancy dessert. This is crispy on the outside and soft on the inside, and it's so good. It tastes like banana bread.

Tip: To test if the oil is hot enough use a wooden spoon and place the bottom of the handle into the oil and if it bubbles around it— it's ready. The oil should reach about 350 to 375 degree F when deep frying— use a candy thermometer.

Makes about 12 fritters.

YUMMY, YUMMY, YUMMY, I GOT LOVE IN MY TUMMY.

BANANA BREAD

This is one of the best banana breads you will ever come across. The best thing about it is it's so easy to prepare. So from me to you, enjoy! This is pictured on pg 83. ♥

- 1 cup of unsalted butter or unsalted margarine (room temperature)
- $\frac{1}{2}$ cup of sugar – if you like it sweet add $\frac{3}{4}$ cup
- 4 medium ripe bananas (mashed)
- 2 large eggs
- 2 teaspoons of vanilla
- 2 cups of white (All purpose) flour sifted
- $2\frac{1}{2}$ teaspoons of baking powder
- $1\frac{1}{2}$ teaspoons of baking soda
- $\frac{1}{2}$ teaspoon of salt
- 1 teaspoon of nutmeg
- $2\frac{1}{2}$ teaspoons of cinnamon
- $1\frac{1}{2}$ teaspoons of lime juice **(optional)**

COOKING AND PREPARATION INSTRUCTIONS

STEP 1. Preheat oven to 350 degrees. In a large bowl or a large sheet of parchment paper add flour, baking powder, baking soda, salt, nutmeg and cinnamon. Set aside.

STEP 2. In a mixer bowl add butter and sugar; mix on medium speed until light and fluffy. (You can do this by hand). Then add the eggs and mix until nice and creamy. Add the mashed bananas and lime and mix until incorporated.

STEP 3. Add the flour into the mixture and mix until combined **(do not over mix)**.

STEP 4. Grease a loaf pan (9 x 5- inch), pour in batter, and bake for about 40–60 minutes or until tester comes out clean.

This batter is also great to make muffins small, medium or large. Baking times will vary, small about 10 minutes, medium 15 minutes and large 20 minutes. Check with a toothpick as mentioned above in step 5. I add chocolate chips, and I tell you, they disappear within minutes. Kids love them and so do adults.

You can add chocolate chunks or nuts or both.

To test if is done, insert a toothpick or raw spaghetti in the middle of the bread or cake; if it comes out clean, it's done.

Tip: If cake looks like it's getting too brown on top and it's still not cooked, cover with foil and continue to bake.

MOBAY OATMEAL COOKIES

In my opinion there is nothing better than a batch of freshly baked cookies. This is such an easy oatmeal recipe jazzed up with some extra special goodies. The aroma of these little babies will have everyone gathered in your kitchen. Good luck and may the kitchen force be with you. This is pictured on pg 83. ❤

- ¾ cup of unsalted butter or unsalted margarine (room temperature)
- 1¼ cup of brown sugar (if you like it sweeter you can use 1½ cup)
- 2 large eggs
- 2 teaspoons of vanilla
- 1½ cups of cake and pastry flour -sifted
- 2½ cups of rolled oats
- 1 teaspoon of baking soda
- ½ teaspoon of salt
- 1 teaspoon of nutmeg
- 2 teaspoons of cinnamon
- 2 cups of chocolate chunks
- ½ cup of sweetened shredded coconut
- 1 cup of chopped pecans

STEP 1. Preheat oven to 375 degrees. On a large sheet of parchment paper or in a large bowl add the four, oatmeal, cinnamon, nutmeg, baking soda, cornstarch, chocolate chunks, coconut flakes and pecans. Set aside

STEP 2. In a mixing bowl add butter and brown sugar and mix on medium speed until creamy about 5 minutes. Add the vanilla and eggs and continue to mix on medium speed until really creamy and fluffy about 5-7 minutes. This is my trick to a really good cookie. ☺

STEP 3. On low speed add the flour mixture from above until combined. **Do not over mix.**

STEP 4. Drop tablespoonful onto a greased or parchment-lined baking sheet and bake for 7 to 12 minutes, until cookies start to brown around the edges and loose their shine.

Cookies will keep up to a week in an airtight container.
Yield: 2 dozen cookies.

Tip: The dough may also be made and frozen in advance and baked as needed.

CHOCOLATE BANANA SQUARES

I have to say, banana cake is one of my favorites and also a big favorite with kids. They devour it really fast, which is good for me; that way I don't eat the entire thing.

- $\frac{3}{4}$ cup unsalted margarine or unsalted butter (room temperature)
- 1 1/3 cup of granulated sugar
- 2 large eggs
- 3 medium ripe bananas (mashed)
- 1 teaspoon of vanilla
- 2 cups of white (All purpose) flour sifted
- $1\frac{1}{2}$ teaspoons of cinnamon and nutmeg
- $\frac{1}{2}$ teaspoon of salt
- $2\frac{1}{2}$ teaspoons of baking powder
- $1\frac{1}{2}$ teaspoon of baking soda
- $2\frac{1}{2}$ cups of buttermilk (2%)
- 2 cups of milk chocolate chunk or chips

COOKING AND PREPARATION INSTRUCTIONS

STEP 1.   Preheat oven to 350 degrees. In a large bowl add flour, cinnamon, nutmeg, salt, baking powder, soda; set aside.

STEP 2.   Add the granulated sugar and butter in a large mixer bowl and mix on medium speed until light and fluffy.

STEP 3.   Add eggs to the butter mixture, mixing until really creamy. In a bowl add the mashed bananas and the milk chocolate chunks; set aside.

STEP 4.   Add milk and flour to the butter mixture until combined then add bananas and mix until incorporated. Do not over mix.

STEP 5.   Pour batter into a greased square 9.5 x 13.5-inch pan; make sure to spread batter evenly in the pan. Bake for 30–60 minutes or until tester comes out clean. Cool and cut

Top with powdered sugar or you can spread or you can drizzle the ganache from page 142.

CHOCOLATE CAKE

I promise you, this will be one of the moistest cakes you've ever had, and the added touch of cinnamon really makes this cake a step ahead of the ordinary chocolate cake. A sweet indulgence and well worth every calorie. And so easy to make, it is fool proof, trust me. This is pictured on pg 83. ❤

- 1 cup of unsalted butter
- 1 2/3 cups of granulated sugar
- 2 large eggs
- 1 teaspoon of vanilla
- 2 cups of white (All purpose) flour sifted
- ¾ cup of unsweetened cocoa powder sifted
- 2½ teaspoons of baking powder
- 1½ teaspoon of baking soda
- 1 teaspoon of salt
- 2 teaspoons of cinnamon (optional)
- 1 cup of semisweet chocolate chips or chunks
- 3 cups of buttermilk + **1/3 cup of 2 % or homo milk for step 1**

COOKING AND PREPARATION INSTRUCTIONS

STEP 1.   Preheat oven to 350 degrees. Melt semisweet, and **1/3 cup of milk** in the microwave for 58 seconds; mix well and cool.

STEP 2.   In a separate bowl combine the flour, cocoa, baking powder, baking soda, salt, and cinnamon. Set aside.

STEP 3.   Add butter and sugar in a large mixer bowl and mix on medium speed until light and fluffy about 5 minutes.

STEP 4.   Add vanilla and eggs and mix on medium speed for 5 more minutes. It should be very creamy. Add the melted chocolate and mix for 1 more minute.

STEP 5.   Add buttermilk and then the flour to the butter mixture and mix on low speed until combined. Batter will be thick.

STEP 6.   Pour the batter into a greased 10 -inch spring form baking pan or 10-inch bunt cake pan. Ensure you spread the batter evenly in the pan use a knife if need be.

STEP 7.   Bake for 40–60 minutes or until tester comes clean (when a toothpick inserted in the center comes out clean, it's done.)

Cool cake. Don't worry if the cake cracks; you can hide any imperfections with whipped cream, fresh berries, or frosting.

This batter is also great to make cupcakes small, medium or large. Baking times will vary, small about 10 minutes, medium 15 minutes and large 20 minutes. Check with a toothpick as mentioned above in step 5.

<u>**Quick ganache recipe**</u>

COOKING AND PREPARATION INSTRUCTIONS

STEP 1.   In a bowl combine ¾ cup semi sweet chocolate chips, 1/3 cup of milk chocolate chips with ½ cup of whipping cream or milk; microwave for about 50-65 seconds.

STEP 2.   Remove from microwave and whisk until milk is fully incorporated and ganache is smooth. Allow to cool slightly and pour over cake.

Top with shaved chocolate. Frost with favorite frosting it's up to you.

This batter would make a great Birthday Cake. Cool cake and spread the ganache evenly; top with little candy flowers that can be bought in most cake baking stores or some grocery stores. You can also use your favorite frosting recipe.

 MAKE A WISH!

Serves 6–8 people.

OH MY GOODNESS CARROT CAKE

This is one cake you can't pass by. The combination of the cream cheese frosting and the moist cake makes this irresistible. Yummy and yummy!! This is pictured on pg 83. ♥

- 1¼ cups of unsalted butter or unsalted margarine
- 1¾ cups of brown sugar
- 4 large eggs (beaten)
- 1 teaspoon of vanilla
- 2 cups of white (All purpose) flour
- 1 tablespoon of cinnamon
- 2 teaspoons of nutmeg
- 3 teaspoons of baking powder
- 1 teaspoon of baking soda
- ½ tablespoon of salt
- 3 cups of shredded carrots (uncooked)
- ½ cup of pecans and raisins
- 1 tablespoon of fresh lime juice

COOKING AND PREPARATION INSTUCTIONS

STEP 1. Preheat oven to 350 degrees. In a bowl combine flour, cinnamon, nutmeg, baking powder, baking soda, and salt. Set aside.

STEP 2. Cream butter, brown sugar, vanilla, and eggs in a large mixer bowl on medium speed until light and fluffy.

STEP 3. On low speed add the flour mixture to the butter mixture and mix until incorporated then add carrots, raisins, pecans, and lime juice until combined.

STEP 4. Pour into square 13 x 9 x 2-inch baking pan, 10-inch flute pan, or tube pan, and bake for 30–60 minutes or until tester comes out clean. (When a toothpick, inserted in the center, comes out clean, it is done.) Cool cake.

ICING
- 1 (8-oz.) package of light cream cheese
- 1/3 cup of unsalted butter
- 2½ cups of icing sugar
- 2 tablespoons of lime juice

COOKING AND PREPARATION INSTRUCTIONS

STEP 1. In a bowl mix the cream cheese, lime juice, and butter until smooth. Add icing sugar gradually, until smooth and creamy.

Top the cake with pecans.

This batter is also great to make cupcakes small, medium or large. Baking times will vary, small about 10 minutes, medium 15 minutes and large 20 minutes. Check with a toothpick as mentioned above in step 5.

IRIE CHEESECAKE DELIGHT

Can it get any easier? I say not. This is definitely a good choice for a dessert after a fabulous meal. This is made without stress, and the great thing is, your guests will think you are a culinary chef. No problem, mon; after all, Jamaicans have been living by this saying and it's about time we do too. This is pictured on pg 84.

➢ 2 packages of light cream cheese
➢ 3–4 cups of prepared unsweetened whipped cream (depending on how creamy you want it)
➢ ½ cup of granulated sugar
➢ 1 cup of chopped strawberries, blueberries, or blackberries (your choice; wash and dry well)
➢ 2 teaspoons of Jamaican rum cream **(optional)**
➢ 16 individual sponge cake cups (found in most grocery stores).

COOKING AND PREPARATION INSTRUCTIONS

STEP 1.   In a mixer on medium speed, combine cream cheese and sugar until smooth.
STEP 2.   Add the whipped cream and mix until incorporated; then add fruit and fold in by hand.
STEP 3.   Spoon into sponge cake cup and top with fruit. Refrigerate for 3 hours, or overnight for best results.

To make your own whipped cream, add 2 cups of whipping cream in a mixer on medium speed and mix for 2 minutes, and then increase speed to high, until stiff peaks form; must be thick.

Note: If you can't find the individual sponge cakes, you can use a prepared pound loaf cake or a chocolate swirl pound loaf cake, which are all available in most grocery stores throughout North America.

CAKE VERSION
•   Same ingredients as above; however, use 3 cups of whipped cream
•   1½–2 packaged pound cakes or chocolate swirl pound cakes or any packaged loaf cake (350g)
•   1 (7 or 8-inch) spring form pan

COOKING AND PREPARATION INSTRUCTIONS

STEP 1.   In a mixer on medium speed, combine cream cheese and sugar until smooth.
STEP 2.   Add the whipped cream and mix until incorporated; then add fruit and fold in by hand.
STEP 3.   Slice the cake about ½-inch thick and arrange on the bottom of a 7or 8-inch pan and press down; also arrange on the sides of the pan and again press firmly but gently; you don't want to break the cake as you press.
STEP 4.   Pour half of the cheese mixture over the cake and gently spread evenly; add another layer of sliced cake then add the second half of the cheese mixture; spread evenly. Cover and refrigerate overnight. Decorate with fresh berries.

Serves 8 people.

CHOCOLATE CHEESECAKE WITH RUM CREAM

Chocolate and rum are some of Jamaica's favorite things: bring them together and you've got yourself a treat to soothe even the savage of hearts. This is pictured on pg 82. ♥

- 3 packs of light cream cheese – Room Temperature
- 1½ cups of granulated sugar (if you find 1½ cup too sweet, you can use 1¼ cup)
- ½ cup of plain yogurt
- 2 tablespoons of Jamaican rum cream (original or Irish cream flavor)
- 2 tablespoons cornstarch
- 3 large eggs- Room Temperature
- ½ cup of unsweetened cocoa powder- sifted

- **CHOCOLATE GRAHAM CRUST   OR   OREO CRUMB CRUST**

CHOCOLATE GRAHAM CRUST	OREO CRUMB CRUST
1¼ cups of graham cracker crumbs	1 1/3 cup of Oreo crumbs
¼ cup of sugar	2 tablespoons of sugar
¼ cup of unsalted butter (melted)	1/3 cup of unsalted butter (melted)
1/3 cup of unsweetened cocoa powder	

COOKING AND PREPARATION INSTRUCTIONS

STEP 1. Prepare crust by combining all the ingredients together and pressing them gently into 9-inch spring form pan; set aside (before pressing the crumb mixture into the pan, taste for sugar and add more if it's not sweet enough for you).

STEP 2. Preheat oven to 350 degrees.

STEP 3. Beat cream cheese, sugar, plain yogurt, and rum cream on medium speed until smooth.

STEP 4. Add cornstarch, 1 tablespoon at a time, blending well; add eggs one at a time until smooth. Finally add the cocoa until well combined.

STEP 5. Lightly grease sides of pan as this will help prevent cheesecake from cracking as it cools. Pour cheese mixture over crust and bake in centre of oven for about 40-60 minutes or until set around edge and centre is still jiggly. Turn off oven, open oven door halfway, and leave cake in oven to cool for about 40 minutes. Remove from oven, run knife around edge of pan to loosen cake from sides, and cool completely. Cover with plastic wrap and refrigerate overnight.

SUBSTITUTE JAMAICAN RUM CREAM with Irish cream.

Don't be concerned if the cake cracks after you remove it from the oven. You can decorate with fresh fruits, lots of shaved chocolate topped with icing sugar, and whipped cream. There are many ways to make this dessert look like you worked for hours.

Tip: To avoid cracking you can place the spring form pan in a large shallow baking pan filled with about 1/3 to ½ with hot water and bake for 40-60 minutes set around edge and centre is still jiggly. Make sure you cover the bottom of the spring form pan with foil to avoid water seeping into the pan.

Serves 6–8 people.

EXOTIC FRUIT BAKE

This is so easy to prepare, which suits me fine. I like to find really easy desserts, because it makes dinner parties less stressful. This is so good, so put away the traditional apple and make room for pineapple, mango, blueberry, and strawberry. We still love you, apple, so don't worry too much. I love this so much! This is pictured on pg 84. ♥

- 7 cups of chopped fresh fruits (pineapple, mango, strawberry, and blueberry)
- 3-4 tablespoons of sugar **(optional)**
- 2 teaspoons of cinnamon
- ½ teaspoon of nutmeg
- 1 tablespoon of fresh lime juice
- 4 tablespoons of flour
- 1 cup of rolled oats
- ¾ cup of brown sugar
- 2/3 cup of unsalted butter or unsalted margarine (room temperature)
- ice cream

COOKING AND PREPARATION INSTRUCTIONS

STEP 1. Preheat oven to 350 degrees.

STEP 2. Taste fruits to ensure their sweetness; if not sweet enough, add sugar to Step 3.

STEP 3. In a bowl combine chopped fruits with cinnamon, nutmeg, lime juice and sugar **(optional)** and mix well. Set aside.

STEP 4. In a separate bowl combine rolled oats, brown sugar, and butter, and mix until well combined.

STEP 5. Add the flour to the fruit and mix well and pour the fruit into a 1.5 glass quart bake ware. With your hands add the sugar mixture evenly on top of fruit.

STEP 6. Bake for 20–25 minutes, until top is golden and crispy.

This can be served warm, at room temperature, or cold.

Serve with your favorite ice cream; a good choice would be mango, vanilla, or strawberry; however, I love chocolate. If ice cream isn't your thing, top with whipped cream or serve solo.

Shown here is 1.5 quart bake ware. You can also use an 8 x 8 x 2, or 9 x 9 x 2-inch square glass baking pan.

Serves 4–6 people.

COCONUT CREAM PIE

This is a dessert from the gods of the Islands. I love coconut cream pie. It always reminds me of "Gilligan's Island," and when a friend of mine gave me the recipe many years ago, I fell in love. This is so easy to make—its full proof. Straight from Jamaica, Mon! "Everting Cris." I always feel like Maryanne or Ginger when I make this pie without the tiny, tiny shorts. ❤

GRAHAM CRUMB CRUST
- 1¼ cups of graham crumb
- ¼ cup of unsalted butter
- 1 teaspoon of sugar

COOKING AND PREPARATION FOR CRUMB CRUST

STEP 1.　Combine graham crumbs and sugar with melted butter; mix well and press on the bottom and sides of a 9-inch pie plate. Bake in a 350 degree oven for 10 minutes. Remove from oven and cool, and then fill with coconut cream mixture.

Coconut Custard Cream filling

- 1 cup of granulated sugar
- ½ cup of cornstarch
- ½ teaspoon of salt
- 3 cups of milk (2% fat or 3% fat)
- 3 large eggs (beaten) – place in large bowl
- 2 teaspoons of vanilla
- 2 cups grated coconut (fresh or unsweetened packaged)
- 1½ cups of whipping cream
- 1 tablespoon of granulated sugar
- 9-inch baked pie shell or graham crumbs

COOKING AND PREPARATION INSTRUCTIONS

STEP 1.　In a medium pot combine sugar, cornstarch, and salt then add the milk; stir until a smooth texture is achieved. Bring pot to the stovetop, and on medium to low heat, cook and bring the mixture to a boil, stirring frequently. Continue to cook for 2 more minutes.

STEP 2.　Remove from heat and stir some of the hot mixture into a bowl with the beaten eggs, and then very slowly combine the rest of the eggs back into the saucepan, mixing constantly.

STEP 3.　Return saucepan to stove and cook, stirring frequently over low heat for an additional 8–10 minutes or until a nice, thick, and creamy texture is achieved.

STEP 4.　Pour mixture into a bowl and stir vanilla and grated coconut. Place wax paper directly on filling and refrigerate for 1–2 hours.

STEP 5.　In a mixer on medium speed, mix whipping cream and 1 tablespoon of sugar for 2–3 minutes and increase speed until stiff peaks form.

STEP 6. Add half of the cream into the cool coconut custard mixture and pour into a cooled baked crumb crust or pie shell; refrigerate for 2–4 more hours or overnight for best results. Spread the rest of the whipping cream on top and serve.

Decorate with more shredded coconut and fruit.
To save time, you can buy your favorite prepared whipped cream and pastry pie shell or graham crumb pie shell.

Serves 4–6 people.

COCONUT CREAM PIE

CHOCOLATE CHUNK BANANA BREAD PUDDING

All I have to say is awesome. The smell is intoxicating and the taste is like heaven. ♥

- 1 loaf of fresh white bread (sliced toast bread, crust removed) cubed
- 6 cups of milk
- 1 can of evaporated milk (2%)
- 3 tablespoons of fresh grated nutmeg, or to taste
- 1 tablespoon of cinnamon
- 2 tablespoons of vanilla
- 1 cup of granulated sugar
- 3 large eggs (beaten)
- 3 medium bananas chopped into chunks
- 1½ cup of milk chocolate chunks of chips
- 2–3 tablespoons of unsalted butter

COOKING AND PREPARATION INSTRUCTIONS

STEP 1.   Preheat oven to 350 degrees.
STEP 2.   In a large bowl add beaten eggs, milk, evaporated milk, grated nutmeg, cinnamon, sugar, and vanilla and mix well.
STEP 3.   Add the bread to the mixture and soak for 5–10 minutes; then mix into the bread the milk chocolate chunks and chopped banana.
STEP 4.   Grease a 9.5 x 13.5-inch (3 quart) baking dish and pour in the bread mixture. Bake for approximately 45–60 minutes, or until golden and is no longer wet; should be spongy when touched.

Serve with Crème De Banana Sauce, whipped cream, or drizzle chocolate sauce for a fancy dessert. Serve warm or at room temperature.

TIP: If at anytime during baking you find the pudding is getting too dark on top or if the edges are getting too crispy just cover with foil and continue to cook until done.

CRÈME DE BANANA SAUCE

- ½ cup each of maple syrup and corn syrup
- 2/3 cup of water
- 1 teaspoon of cinnamon
- 1/3 cup of brown sugar
- 2 tablespoons of cornstarch
- 1 oz. of crème de banana

COOKING AND PREPARATION INSTRUCTIONS

STEP 1.   In a small saucepan whisk together maple syrup, corn syrup, water, sugar, cinnamon, and cornstarch; bring to a boil, stirring constantly. Boil for 1 minute and remove from heat. Let cool and pour in Crème De Banana. (Sauce can be covered and refrigerated for up to 3 days.)

BANANA BREAD PUDDING WITH DRIZZLED CHOCOLATE SAUCE

HERE ARE MY TWO BIGGEST FANS. MY SON'S BIG QUESTION MOST
DAYS IS WILL I MAKE HIM BEEF PATTIES, ONE OF HIS FAVORITE
THINGS TO EAT.

BREAD PUDDING

This dessert will remind you of the British rule in Jamaica. This is really very good; a good friend of the family brought forward this recipe. It tastes like French toast to me, which I happen to love. ♥

- 1 loaf of fresh white bread (sliced toast bread, crust removed) cubed
- 6 cups of milk
- 1 can of evaporated milk
- 2 tablespoons of nutmeg, or to taste
- 1 tablespoon of cinnamon
- 1 cup of granulated sugar
- 2 tablespoons of vanilla
- 3 large eggs (beaten)
- 2–3 tablespoons of unsalted butter
- ½ cup of raisins (optional)

COOKING AND PREPARATION INSTRUCTIONS

STEP 1. Preheat oven to 350 degrees.

STEP 2. In a large bowl add beaten eggs, milk, evaporated milk, grated nutmeg, cinnamon, sugar, vanilla, and raisins and mix well. Add the bread to the mixture and soak for 5–10 minutes.

STEP 3. Grease a square 9.5 x 13.5-inch (3 quart) baking dish and pour in bread mixture. Bake for approximately 45–60 minutes, or until golden and is no longer wet.

Serve hot or at room temperature, with whipped cream or Rum Sauce for a fancy dessert, or you can eat as is.

TIP: If at anytime during baking you find the pudding is getting too dark on top or if the edges are getting too crispy just cover with foil and continue to cook until done.

RUM SAUCE

- ½ cup each of maple syrup and corn syrup
- 2/3 cup of water
- 1 teaspoon of cinnamon
- 1/3 cup of brown sugar
- 2 tablespoons of cornstarch
- 1 oz. of rum (**Appleton Jamaica Rum or your choice**)

COOKING AND PREPARATION INSTRUCTIONS

STEP 1. In a small saucepan whisk together maple syrup, corn syrup, water, sugar, cinnamon, and cornstarch; bring to a boil, stirring constantly. Boil for 1 minute and remove from heat. Let cool and pour in rum. (Sauce can be covered and refrigerated for up to 3 days.)

WHO NEEDS A SPA WHEN YOU CAN BATHE ALFRESCO? JUST ASK MY SON ANDREW, ENJOYING HIS BATH—ONLY IN JAMAICA.

SWEET POTATO PUDDING

This is a favorite among the locals, which was passed down from the British settlers, but is distinctly Jamaican. ❤

- ➢ 3 pounds of sweet potatoes (Jamaican sweet potatoes, boniato, also referred to as batata)
- ➢ 1½ cups of brown sugar
- ➢ 3¼ cups of coconut milk (fresh or canned)
- ➢ 1½ cup of white (All purpose) flour
- ➢ 1 teaspoon of nutmeg
- ➢ 1 teaspoon of cinnamon
- ➢ 1 tablespoon of sugar
- ➢ ½ cup of raisins
- ➢ ½ teaspoon of salt
- ➢ 2 teaspoons of unsalted margarine

COOKING AND PREPARATION INSTRUCTIONS

STEP 1. Preheat oven to 350 degrees.

STEP 2. Peel sweet potatoes, wash, and then grate. Place in large bowl and set aside.

STEP 3. In a bowl blend flour, nutmeg, cinnamon, and salt.

STEP 4. Combine the flour mixture to the grated potatoes and mix well.

STEP 5. Add sugar, raisins, and coconut milk; mix well.

STEP 6. Grease a square 13 x 9-inch pan; pour batter in the pan and bake until it sets, about 1-1½ hours. Cool and cut into squares.

TIP: If at anytime during baking you find the pudding is getting too dark on top or if the edges are getting too crispy just cover with foil and continue to cook until done. It's done when the liquid is absorbed at has a nice golden color.

Serves 6–8 people.

IT'S ALWAYS OKAY TO ENJOY YOUR FAVORITE TREATS, NO PROBLEM, MON!

GRILLED PINEAPPLE WITH CHOCOLATE SAUCE

This is so easy and really delicious. This is a nice dessert to end a nice dinner party. ♥

- 6 slices of pineapple, about 1 inch thick
- 2 tablespoons each of brown sugar and cinnamon
- chocolate sauce

COOKING AND PREPARATION INSTRUCTIONS

STEP 1.   Turn barbeque to medium and grease grill to avoid sticking.

STEP 2.   In a large bowl add the pineapple, brown sugar and cinnamon mix well. Grill for 2-5 minutes per side or until soft. You want to achieve grill marks on both sides.

STEP 3.   You can also make fruit kebobs. Cut pineapple into 2 inch chunks and add to a bowl with the brown sugar and cinnamon. Add 4 cubed pineapple per skewer. I also half strawberries. Alternate the pineapple with the strawberry. Grill 2-5 minutes per side or until soft and nice grill marks are achieved.

CHOCOLATE SAUCE

- 1 1/3 cups of milk chocolate chips
- 1/3 cup milk (2% or 3%)
- 1 tablespoon of Jamaican rum cream, or substitute with Irish cream

COOKING AND PREPARATION INSTRUCTIONS

STEP 1.   Combine the chocolate with the milk and microwave for 50–65 seconds or until melted. Stir very well and add the rum cream or Irish cream. You can also melt chocolate with milk over a double boiler on the stovetop.

Note: If you find that the mixture is too thick, add milk 1 tablespoon at a time, and if it's too watery, add more chocolate until you achieve a smooth chocolate sauce.

On an individual plate pour chocolate and put grilled pineapple on top and drizzle with more chocolate. Trust me, this is so good.

Serves 6 people.

EXOTIC FRUIT PLATTER

Fruit is always a nice way to end a dinner party, but why not take it one step further with some chocolate for dipping or a sugar syrup; Jamaican style, of course. ♥

- 1 pineapple (chopped into 1-inch chunks)
- 2 papayas (cut into slices)
- 3 cups of fresh strawberries (halved)
- 2 mangos (cut into cubes)
- 3 cups of watermelon (chopped/cubed)

COOKING AND PREPARATION INSTRUCTIONS

STEP 1.   **Choice A-** Arrange on a platter and serve with chocolate sauce (pg 154); place chocolate sauce in bowl for dipping.
Choice B- If using the sugar syrup, cool first at room temperature and then pour over fruit. Mix well, and refrigerate for 1–2 hours.
Choice C- For a fancy dinner party, place the fruit in a fancy cup or bowl, and then drizzle chocolate sauce or use sugar syrup. Top with whipped cream and a sprig of mint.

SUGAR SYRUP

- $1\frac{1}{2}$ cups of water
- $\frac{1}{2}$ cup of granulated sugar
- 1 tablespoon of lime juice
- 1 teaspoon of rum (**Appleton Jamaica Rum** or your choice)
- 1 cinnamon stick
- 1 tablespoon of chopped mint

COOKING AND PREPARATION INSTRUCTIONS

STEP 1.   In a small pot combine all ingredients and cook down for 20 minutes on medium heat; let stand at room temperature, and then pour on fruit; mix well and refrigerate for 1–2 hours.

Serves 4 people.

EASTER BUN

Traditionally made at Easter, hence the name; and it's served with Jamaican cheese. This requires more work, but don't panic; you only need to make it once a year. This is easy to double, and it's nice to make during the holidays to give your family and friends a freshly baked gift. ♥

- ½ cups of raisins
- 2 tablespoons of yeast
- ¼ cup of luke warm water
- ½ cup of warm milk
- 1 teaspoon of molasses
- 1 teaspoon of browning (**Grace products,** sold in most grocery stores in North America or in West Indian stores)
- 1/3 cup of unsalted butter
- 2½ cups of white (All purpose) flour
- 1 cup of brown sugar
- ½ teaspoon of ground dried ginger
- 1 teaspoon of grated nutmeg
- 1½ teaspoons of cinnamon
- 1 teaspoon of salt
- 1 large egg (beaten)
- sugar glaze (see below for instructions)

COOKING AND PREPARATION INSTRUCTIONS

STEP 1.   In a small bowl dilute yeast in warm water. Also in a large bowl combine flour, brown sugar, ground ginger, nutmeg, and salt. Set aside.

STEP 2.   In another small bowl melt butter, and cool. In a separate bowl add warm milk, molasses, and browning.

STEP 3.   To the flour mixture add the melted butter, milk mixture, egg, and yeast mixture and mix until well combined. At this stage add the raisins.

STEP 4.   Dough will be sticky, mix with a wooden spoon for several minutes to work the glutens. Pour into a buttered loaf pan. Cover and let rise for 2–4 hours or until it doubles.

STEP 5.   Bake in a 350 degree oven for about 35 minutes; remove and brush with glaze, and continue to bake for 5–10 more minutes or until tester comes out clean (when toothpick is inserted in the center and comes out clean). It may look dry when you cut into it, but you will be pleasantly surprised at how moist it is.

<u>If necessary cover the bun with foil to stop over browning.</u>

SUGAR GLAZE
- 2 tablespoons of sugar
- ¼ cup of water

COOKING AND PREPARATION INSTRUCTIONS

STEP 1.   In bowl add sugar and water, and mix well.

EASTER BUN AND CHEESE

ALL ELEMENTS OF JAMAICA GIVE SWEET LIFE. SHOWN HERE ARE
MY COUSIN MATTHEW, MY NEPHEW SAM, AND NIECE SAMANTHA.

SPICED BREAD

Not to be confused with Easter Bun on page 180; however, it's very similar, but this is much easier to make no stress baking. ♥

- 3 cups of white (All purpose) flour
- 3 teaspoons of baking powder
- 1 cup of brown sugar
- 2 large eggs (beaten)
- 1½ tablespoons of pure vanilla or browning
- 2/3 cup of unsalted butter or unsalted margarine melted (cooled)
- 2 cups of milk (2%)
- 1 tablespoon of cinnamon and nutmeg
- ½–1 cup of raisins or ½–1 cup or chocolate chunks.

COOKING AND PREPARATION INSTRUCTIONS

STEP 1.   Add all the ingredients in a large bowl and mix well either by hand or with a mixer Pour mixture into a greased loaf pan (9 X 5-inch) and bake in a 350 degree oven for 40–60 minutes, or until tester comes out clean.

TOTO

This is a very moist cake with a muffin like texture. If you like coconut, then this is the treat for you. Sing it to me sister. ♥

- 1¼ cups of brown sugar
- 1 cup of unsalted butter or unsalted margarine (softened)
- 2 large eggs
- 1 tablespoon of browning (found in most grocery stores)
- 3 cups of white (All purpose) flour sifted
- 3 teaspoons of baking powder
- 1 teaspoon of baking soda
- ½ teaspoon of salt
- 1 teaspoon of nutmeg
- 1½ teaspoons of cinnamon
- 1½ cups of milk (2%)
- 1½ cups of shredded coconut (sweetened)

COOKING AND PREPARATION INSTRUCTIONS

STEP 1. Preheat oven to 350 degrees. In a large bowl or large sheet of parchment paper add flour, baking soda, baking powder, salt, nutmeg, cinnamon, and shredded coconut and set aside.

STEP 2. In a large mixer bowl add sugar and butter and mix on medium speed until light and fluffy. Add eggs and browning until well combined.

STEP 3. Next add milk and then flour mixture to the butter mixture, mixing on low speed until combined (do not over mix).

STEP 4. Pour into greased 13 x 9 x 2-inch baking pan or a 10-inch square baking pan and spread evenly , and bake for about 30–60 minutes or until tester comes out clean.

STEP 5. Allow to cool. Top with grated milk chocolate, icing sugar or cream cheese frosting, pg 142

This batter is also great to make cupcakes small, medium or large. Baking times will vary, small about 10 minutes, medium 15 minutes and large 20 minutes. Check with a toothpick as mentioned above in step 5.

CARROT PUNCH

- 1 cup carrot juice
- 1½ cups of condensed milk
- ½ teaspoon of grated nutmeg
- 2 cups of beer

PREPARATION INSTRUCTIONS

STEP 1.   Mix juice with condensed milk and nutmeg.
STEP 2.   Add beer and serve chilled over ice.

CARROT DRINK

- 6 large carrots
- 1 cup of water
- 1¼ cups of granulated sugar
- 1½ cups of milk (2% fat)
- ½ cup of condensed milk
- ½ teaspoon of nutmeg
- 2 tablespoons of lime juice

PREPARATION INSTRUCTIONS

STEP 1.   Grate the carrots in a blender or food processor. Add water and press carrots through a sieve.
STEP 2.   Strain and add the lime juice to the carrot juice.
STEP 3.   Add the sugar, nutmeg, milk, and condensed milk; mix well. Chill and serve.

CHEERS! WE ARE ALWAYS HAPPY WITH A DRINK OR TWO.

SORREL

This is traditionally served at Christmas, because the sorrel plants bloom just before the Christmas season. Fresh sorrel is imported in early December and can be found in markets that carry Caribbean produce. I, myself, have never made it; I've only seen it being made.

- $3\frac{1}{2}$ dozen of fresh sorrel sepals (found in West Indian stores)
- 3 tablespoons of fresh ginger (chopped)
- 8 cups of boiling water
- $1\frac{1}{2}$ cups of brown sugar
- $\frac{1}{2}$ cup of sugar
- $\frac{1}{2}$ cup of Jamaican white rum (**Wray and Nephew White Overproof Rum** or your choice)
- 3 limes

PREPARATION INSTRUCTIONS

STEP 1.   Strip off the red sepals and discard the buds. Combine the sepals with the ginger in a large bowl.

STEP 2.   Squeeze the juice of the limes and add the lime peels to the bowl and let stand for a few hours to a full day.

STEP 3.   Strain the mixture and sweeten with both sugars and add the rum. Chill and serve.

SIMPLE SYRUP

This is used to make many drinks, and is easy to double. Remember, it's always 2 parts sugar to 1 part water.

- 1 cup of water
- 2 cups of sugar
- 1 tablespoon of corn syrup

PREPARATION INSTRUCTIONS

STEP 1.   Add the water, corn syrup, and sugar in a small saucepan; mix well. On medium heat, bring sugar mixture to a boil, stirring constantly.

STEP 2.   Reduce heat and continue to cook until sugar is fully dissolved.

STEP 3.   Remove from heat and cool completely. Pour mixture into a covered container and refrigerate. This can be stored indefinitely.

This yields approximately $1\frac{1}{2}$ cups.

PINA COLADA

- 2 cups of chunked pineapple
- 3 oz. of pina colada syrup
- 1 oz. of coconut rum
- $\frac{1}{2}$ oz. of gold rum (**Appleton Jamaica Rum** or your choice), or white rum

PREPARATION INSTRUCTIONS

STEP 1.   In a blender add all ingredients with crushed ice until well blended.

JAMAICAN FRUIT PUNCH

- 2 cups of pineapple juice
- 1 cup of fresh pineapple (cubed)
- $\frac{1}{2}$ cup of orange juice
- $\frac{1}{2}$ cup of lemon juice
- 1 1/3 cups of water
- 1 teaspoon of ground allspice
- $\frac{1}{2}$ teaspoon of nutmeg
- 2 tablespoons of honey
- 3 cups of ginger ale
- 1 cup of soda water
- ice

PREPARATION INSTRUCTIONS

STEP 1.   Mix all the ingredients in a punch bowl and then add ginger ale.
STEP 2.   Add crushed ice and ENJOY!

TROPICAL PUNCH

- 1 cup of lime or lemon juice
- 4 cups of orange juice
- 8 cups of water
- 3 cups of grapefruit juice
- 4 cups of pineapple juice
- $\frac{1}{2}$ cup of strawberry syrup
- $1\frac{1}{4}$ cups of simple syrup (see pg 188)
- 1 cup of fresh pineapple (chopped into chunks)
- 7 cups of ginger ale
- 1 cup of club soda

PREPARATION INSTRUCTIONS

STEP 1.   In a big bowl mix all the ingredients together and then add ginger ale and club soda.
STEP 2.   Add ice and serve.

NO PROBLEM

- ½ oz. of lime juice
- 1½ oz. of fruit juice
- 1½ oz. of pineapple juice
- 1½ oz. of orange juice
- 1½ oz. of strawberry syrup
- 1 oz. of coconut rum
- ½ oz. crème de banana
- ice

PREPARATION INSTRUCTIONS

STEP 1.   In a martini shaker add all the ingredients; mix very well.

STEP 2.   Pour into a glass with plenty of ice.

STRAWBERRY AND BANANA FROZEN DAIQUIRI

- 2 cups of strawberry-banana juice (any brand, found in most grocery stores)
- 1 cup of frozen strawberries
- 1 oz. of crème de banana
- 1 oz. of strawberry syrup
- 1–2 oz. of gold rum (**Appleton Jamaica Rum** or your choice), or white rum
- 1 cup of crushed ice

PREPARATION INSTRUCTIONS

STEP 1.   In a blender add juice, frozen strawberries, crème de banana, strawberry syrup, ice, and rum, until well blended.

STEP 2.   Pour into a nice glass and garnish with fresh strawberry or banana.

SLUSHY TROPICAL FRUIT DRINK

- 1 cup of frozen pineapple
- 1 cup of frozen strawberries
- 1 cup of strawberry-banana juice
- ½ cup of pineapple juice
- ice

PREPARATION INSTRUCTIONS

STEP 1. Combine all ingredients in a blender and blend until smooth.

STEP 2. Pour into a tall glass and garnish with fresh strawberry or pineapple.

For more of a kick add 1 oz. of rum.

BANANA COLADA

- 2 medium bananas (you can use 1½ banana; it's up to you)
- 1½ oz. of gold (**Appleton Jamaica Rum** or your choice) or white rum
- ½ oz. of crème de banana
- 1 tablespoon of lime juice
- 2 oz. of pina colada syrup
- crushed ice

PREPARATION INSTRUCTIONS

STEP 1. Blend all ingredients, including ice, until well combined.

STEP 2. Pour in a tall glass and garnish with fresh banana.

VIRGIN ISLAND

- 1 cup of canned or fresh pineapple (chopped)
- 1¼ cups of pineapple juice
- 3 tablespoons of coconut milk
- 2 tablespoons of lemon juice
- 1 oz. of strawberry syrup
- ice

PREPARATION INSTRUCTIONS

STEP 1.   Place all ingredients in a blender and blend until smooth.
STEP 2.   Pour into a fancy glass with ice. Decorate glass with fresh pineapple slice and lemon slice.

JAMAICAN BANANA PUNCH

- ½ cup of simple syrup (see pg 188
- 1 teaspoon of ground nutmeg
- 1 teaspoon of ground cinnamon
- ½ cup of soda water
- 1½ cups of gold rum (**Appleton Jamaica Rum** or your choice) or white rum
- 3 cups of banana liquor
- 4 cups of pineapple juice
- 4 cups of orange juice
- 4 cups of lemon juice
- ½ cup of ginger ale
- 1 cup each of sliced oranges and pineapple chunks
- ice

PREPARATION INSTRUCTIONS

STEP 1.   Place simple syrup, nutmeg, and cinnamon in a jug; add soda water and stir very well.
STEP 2.   Place ice cubes in a large punch bowl and add rum, liquor, pineapple juice, orange juice, and lemon juice.
STEP 3.   Add soda water mixture, ginger ale, and fruit to the punch bowl; mix gently and serve.

THAT'S ME, IN ONE OF MY MOST FAVORITE PLACES IN THE WORLD, JAMAICA.

IT'S ALL ABOUT TIME!

HERE IS A LIST OF MY FAVORITE PLACES TO STAY, IF YOU EVER GET THE CHANCE TO VISIT THE LOVELY JAMAICA.

SANDALS RESORTS- My favorite would be Sandals Dunn's River, but they are all beautiful! (Nice for a honeymoon or special occasion, couples only.)

RUI- We spent two days on this resort, located in Negril, on a beautiful beach; part of the 7-mile beach that is amazing. Negril is laid back and a nice place for kids and the scenery is beautiful.

RENAISSANCE JAMAICA- This is the place to be if you like action. This is located in the heart of Ocho Rios, footsteps to the hustle and bustle. They also have a nightclub on the resort (Jamic'n me crazy), which happens to be the most popular disco in the area.

BEACHES NEGRIL- We only paid one visit to this property to see what it looks like, and it's beautiful. It's gorgeous; I must save up for this trip, because I know it will be worth it. (Located in Negril, this is part of the Sandals Resort, but it caters to families).

Also nice is **POINT VILLAGE** IN NEGRIL, AND **SANDCASTLES** IN OCHO RIOS.

On my next trip, I have to include a visit to Port Antonio, apparently the most beautiful part of the Island, frequented by many celebrities. Many films have been shot on location, such as "Cocktail," "Blue Lagoon," and "Lord of the Flies." Somewhat expensive, but it's always nice to dream.

Although English is the official language of Jamaica, most likely you will hear something that sounds strange or even foreign. The language is what is referred to as patois. Patois combines English, Spanish, Portuguese, and African phrases, which sounds unusual to most of us and most difficult to understand.

Here are a few catchphrases that you can impress your guests with:

- what a gwaan (what is going on?)
- yow ah weh yuh-a-duh? (hey, what are you doing?)
- comm yah (come here)
- tek care a yuhself (take care of yourself)
- si yuh lata (see you later)
- everyting cris (everything is ok)
- mi soon cum back (I will be back soon)
- how yuh doin'? (how are you doing?)
- wahpen'? (what's up?)
- mi love chaklit cake with nuff icenin (I love chocolate cake with plenty of icing)
- mil like yuh cris cyar (I like your new car)
- she a mi bess bess fren (she is my best friend)
- how yuh nyam summuch (how do you eat so much?)

For a fun dinner buffet, any time of the year:

Include fresh fruits as decorations along with exotic fresh flowers on your buffet table.
Be sure to include favorites **like jerk chicken, beef patties, ribs, festivals, oxtail stew, rice and peas, coleslaw, potato salad, salt fish balls, carrot cake, exotic fruit bake, as well as fresh fruit for dessert—your choice; and you have lots to choose from.**

The beauty of this menu is that you can prepare the beef patties and salt fish balls ahead of time, cook, and freeze. Pop in the oven when ready to use.

The meats should be marinated the night before. Make the coleslaw and potato salad the night before and refrigerate. The desserts can be made the night before as well. All you have to do is cook the meat the following day and make the rice and peas, so you'll have lots of time for yourself.

Make sure to have reggae playing in the background for the full effect. Here is a list of good reggae singers: Bob Marley, Beanie man, Bounty Killa, Shaggy, Lady Saw, and Shawn Paul, to mention only a few. There are great CDs on mainstream reggae, which you can find in most music stores throughout North America.

CODFISH BALLS, BEEF PATTIES, STIR FRIED NOODLES, AND OVEN ROASTED RIBS; IN THE BACK WE HAVE RICE AND PEAS, AND EXOTIC FRUIT IN A PINEAPPLE—ALL TO ENJOY!

SHOWN HERE ARE SOME OF MY SMILING FAMILY MEMBERS, ENJOYING COFFEE AFTER ANOTHER BIG MEAL. MY MOM, DAD, COUSIN FRANK, LORI, FATHER-IN-LAW CHARLES, CHRIS, JODY, AND VERA.

FORMAL DINNER PARTY MENU IDEAS

#1
   Appetizer: crab salad in papaya
   Soup: callaloo and crab soup
   Main course: grilled salmon with grilled plantain
   Dessert: grilled pineapple with chocolate sauce

#2
   Appetizer: grilled shrimp with papaya sauce
   Soup: pureed pumpkin soup
   Main course: roast beef with Island love mashed sweet potatoes
   Dessert: banana bread pudding topped with crème de banana sauce

#3
   Appetizer: curry fish cakes with mango and papaya chutney
   Main course: oxtail stew with rice and peas and festival
    Dessert: exotic fruit bake topped with ice cream

Enjoy any of the above and many more.

Here is a list of restaurants in Jamaica that I love. If you are ever in Jamaica, I hope you get a chance to experience them too.

Ocho Rios Village Jerk Center – Located in Ocho Rios
It's an open-air concept and casual dining atmosphere. It is just the perfect setting for great jerk dishes, and don't worry; if it gets too hot, you can cool yourself down with red stripe beer or a cool fruit drink.

Parkway Restaurant - Located in Ocho Rios
Although plain and unassuming, this casual spot is a perfect place to eat as the Jamaicans do. You will enjoy great traditional dishes. Just don't be surprised if the place is crowded.

Windies – Located in Ocho Rios (Dunn's River Resort)
Reservations are required. Serves delicious West Indian food with a flare and all done in an elegant atmosphere. You can't go wrong with any of its creative and mouthwatering dishes.

Island Grill – Located in Montego Bay
Serves up great Jamaican dishes prepared in a healthier fashion, but don't get too concerned; it still has all the great taste that one expects from Jamaican cuisine.

Jade Garden - Located in Kingston
This restaurant has incredible views of the mountains, and serves up delicious Chinese cuisine. The sweet and sour pork is awesome; the best I've ever had. You can't go wrong with any of its dishes.

SMILING FACES ALWAYS IN JAMAICA, CELEBRATING AUNTIE SANNIE'S BIRTHDAY.

In Negril you will see one of the most beautiful sunsets in the world.

Since I know there is little chance of me winning an Oscar, this is probably my only opportunity to thank my peeps (people), so bear with me. One good thing about this is I don't have to worry about the music cutting me off. So here goes ...

I have to thank my husband, Steve, for his support; I couldn't have done this without him. I couldn't have imagined doing this before I met him. His encouragement was exactly what I needed; this gave me the confidence to complete my dream. Of course, there were many perks for him, like the many great meals. I had to test my recipes and take pictures, and sometimes more than once. Although he has complained of weight gain, hey, I didn't force him; he wanted to eat all that food. I also want to thank my mom, dad , sister, Lina, brother-in-law, Vito, brother, Vito, sister-in-law, Lori, mother-in-law, Marcia, father-in-law, Charles, sister-in-law, Jody, my nieces and nephews, Elisabeth, Samantha, Sam, and Nicholas, and last but not least, Connie Roti, and all who helped me with different aspects of my book and dream. Thanks, family, for putting up with me and handling my Martha Stewart moments. Special thanks go to my son, who made me see the world in a different way. His laughter is like angels singing on the horizon, and all my problems melt away when I see him. Dreams are for sharing, and with my family, I will see the sun shine bright as though the gods were shinning down on me. I cannot finish without thanking my two angels who have given me more motivation and desire than I could have asked for: my late brother Frank, who I wish could be part of this, but I know he is with me every moment and through every journey I take. He was one of the funniest people I have ever known, and a fabulous cook. I also need to thank Nanny, who showed me that Jamaican food is about a feeling that the rest of the world needs to know about; and for all her stories, which kept me fascinated every day by her front yard. Angels do exist; you just have to look in the right spots. Open your eyes and enjoy the beauty around you; enjoy each and every day. After all, it's about time.